Zen and the Art of Medical Ethics

A Mindful Approach to Healthcare

Dominic M. Etli, DNP

Zen and the Art of Medical Ethics:
A Mindful Approach to Healthcare
Dominic M. Etli, DNP
ALL RIGHTS ARE RESERVED.

ISBN: 9798863422329
Lifeline Press

www.ethicalconsent.org

DEDICATION

To Harald,

Your guidance lit the path during my most crucial years of ethical development. More than just imparting knowledge, you led by example. Your words instructed, but your actions inspired.

You understood that shaping young hearts and minds requires as much patience as rigor. You were quick to praise yet slow to judge. And you cared for each student as an individual on their own journey.

From you, I learned that education at its best is not a monologue but a dialogue - an exchange of ideas to uncover truth together. Your mind remained open, even as your principles stood firm.

Your lessons equipped me with the tools to navigate difficulties ethically and find meaning in them. Thanks to you, I walk with courage, serve with empathy, and lead with honor.

Above all, you've shown me that carefully nurtured wisdom endures well beyond formal education. Your guiding voice serves as a lasting moral compass, propelling me onward.

With deep gratitude,

Dominic

CONTENTS

ACKNOWLEDGMENTS

First and foremost, I'd like to express my profound gratitude to my beautiful family. Thank you for your unwavering support, and your patience during those long nights when I was writing and rewriting. You are my bedrock, and this book would not have been possible without you.

To my friends, thank you for the laughter, the sanity checks, and the much-needed breaks that reminded me there's life outside the pages of a manuscript. Your camaraderie provided the positivity that fueled my writing process.

I'd also like to thank my mentors and colleagues for their invaluable input and for the stimulating discussions that sparked many of the ideas explored in this book. Your wisdom and insight have been instrumental in shaping my thoughts and perspectives.

Finally, I would like to acknowledge the readers. Your openness to new ideas and your hunger for knowledge are the reasons why writers like me continue to write. May this book provide you with the enlightenment you seek, and may it serve as a starting point on your journey of understanding and growth.

Thank you all. This book is a testament to the fact that writing is never a solitary endeavor.

Introduction

'It is a good viewpoint to see the world as a dream. When you have something like a nightmare, you will wake up and tell yourself that it was only a dream. It is said that the world we live in is not a bit different from this.'

When I was 17, my Sensei handed me the Hagakure, and it was like being given a treasure map to the soul of the samurai. But this wasn't just about martial arts; it was a philosophical compass that pointed toward a life of ethical rigor. Fast forward to today, and I find myself in the trenches of healthcare—a battlefield of its own, fraught with ethical landmines and moral complexities. The stakes? Nothing less than the sanctity of human life.

This book is the culmination of that journey, a fusion of ancient samurai wisdom and modern medical ethics. It's an exploration, a dialogue between two worlds that, at first glance, seem worlds apart but are bound by the same ethical imperatives. It's my attempt to serve as a bridge between the warrior's honor and the healer's compassion, between the samurai's blade and the clinician's acumen. So, let's embark on this quest together, wielding the Hagakure as our guide, as we navigate the ethical labyrinths of healthcare with the precision and integrity of a samurai.

Imagine you're standing at the edge of a cliff, staring into an abyss of ethical dilemmas and life-altering decisions. Welcome to the world of healthcare—a realm where every choice you make reverberates through the lives of your patients, their families, and even your own soul. Now, what if I told you that the wisdom of ancient samurai could be your guiding light in this labyrinth? Sounds like a plot twist straight out of a Toshiro Mifune film, doesn't it? But stay with me; this is a journey worth taking.

Hagakure

"The world is but a dream," says the Hagakure, a text penned by Yamamoto Tsunetomo, a samurai turned Zen monk. This 18th-century manuscript, originally shared only among an elite circle of warriors, is a treasure trove of wisdom "Hidden by the Leaves." It's like a secret recipe passed down through generations, each ingredient a virtue—courage, honor, loyalty, wisdom—that can elevate your life, and yes, your medical practice, to the realm of the extraordinary.

The Hagakure, an enigmatic guidebook for samurais, serves as a bridge between Zen and Bushido. It's like an interdisciplinary team meeting where different specialties come together to discuss a complex case. The Hagakure offers practical wisdom that's surprisingly relevant to healthcare, like a vintage stethoscope that works just as well as its modern counterparts. It teaches us to be decisive yet mindful, loyal yet ethical, courageous yet compassionate; qualities that are as essential in navigating the labyrinthine corridors of a hospital as they are in the battlefield or the monastery.

Why should a healthcare provider, care about Zen and Bushido? Because these ancient philosophies offer timeless insights that can serve as ethical compasses in our modern medical landscape. They're like the foundational courses in medical school that you never knew you needed but will continually refer back to throughout your career.

Zen and Bushido: A Brief Overview

Zen and Bushido—two ancient Eastern philosophies that seem as distant from a modern hospital as a tranquil Zen Garden is from a bustling ER. But are they really? Let's dig a little deeper and unearth the gems hidden in these age-old teachings, shall we?

Zen, a philosophy that flourished in ancient Japan, is like the calming breath you take before making a difficult diagnosis. It's the philosophy that teaches us to be fully present, to embrace the here and now as if it were a fragile vial of life-saving medication. Mindfulness, simplicity, and interconnectedness are its core tenets. Imagine applying this to healthcare: being fully present during patient consultations, simplifying complex treatment plans, and recognizing the interconnectedness of physical, emotional, and social factors in patient care. It's like the holistic approach to medicine that we often aspire to but rarely achieve.

Now, let's pivot to Bushido, often dubbed the "Way of the Warrior." If Zen is the calming breath, then Bushido is the steady hand that performs a surgical procedure with unwavering precision. Originating from the samurai class of feudal Japan, Bushido is a code of conduct that's as structured as a well-organized patient chart. It emphasizes virtues like loyalty, honor, and courage—virtues that are not just ornamental but functional, like the essential instruments in a surgical toolkit. Imagine being a healthcare provider guided by these principles. Your loyalty isn't just to your job but to the ethical standards of your profession. Your honor reflects not just your reputation but your commitment to patient welfare. Your courage is manifested not in grand gestures but in everyday ethical decisions, like choosing the right treatment despite external pressures.

Why Samurai Wisdom is Relevant to Medical Ethics

It's a fair question. After all, the samurai lived in a world far removed from the sterile halls of modern hospitals and the intricate algorithms of medical diagnostics. But here's the kicker: the principles that guided these ancient warriors are as relevant to your daily ethical challenges as a well-calibrated MRI machine is to modern diagnostics.

Decisiveness, for instance, is like the swift administration of an antivenom after a snakebite. In healthcare, hesitation can be lethal. Whether you're deciding on a treatment plan or prioritizing tasks in a busy clinic, the ability to make quick, informed decisions is crucial. The samurai understood this well; their lives often depended on the blade of a sword swung in the space of a heartbeat. Your "sword" might be a scalpel, a prescription pad, or a difficult conversation, but the principle remains the same: act swiftly but wisely.

Embracing challenges is another samurai virtue that translates seamlessly into healthcare. Think of it as the resilience you muster when faced with a complicated case or an ethical dilemma. It's like being handed a patient chart filled with multiple comorbidities and conflicting medications, and instead of feeling overwhelmed, you see it as a puzzle to be solved, a challenge to be met head-on.

Resolve, in the samurai context, is the unwavering commitment to see things through to the end. In healthcare, it's akin to the dedication you show when managing a long-term patient or navigating the complexities of end-of-life care. It's the emotional and ethical stamina that keeps you going, like a marathon runner pushing through the last grueling miles.

Loyalty and honor might sound like archaic terms, but in healthcare, they're as current as pagers and fax machines, which hospitals still use daily for reasons I cannot fathom. Your loyalty isn't just to your institution but to your patients and ethical principles. It's like the Hippocratic Oath etched into your professional DNA. Honor, on the other hand, is your commitment to uphold these principles, even when it's inconvenient or challenging. It's the ethical backbone that keeps you upright when the winds of medical politics and bureaucracy try to bend you.

Mindfulness, a cornerstone of both Zen and samurai philosophy, is like the keen observation skills you employ during patient assessments, even when there's a shouting match happening in the room next door. It's the ability to be fully present, to notice the subtle signs and symptoms that could easily be overlooked, and to listen—really listen—to your patients.

And let's not forget the delicate balance between compassion and justice. In healthcare, this is often the tightrope you walk when allocating limited resources or making triage decisions. It's like being the conductor of a complex medical orchestra, ensuring that each section—be it patient care, resource allocation, or ethical considerations—plays in harmony.

Enlightened Path

The number seven symbolizes completeness in Zen

Buddhism. It's no coincidence that this book is structured into seven chapters, each serving as a stepping stone on our journey through the rich landscape of Hagakure wisdom and its modern-day relevance to medical ethics. Think of each chapter as a different department in a hospital, each with its own unique set of challenges, ethical dilemmas, and opportunities for growth.

Sprinkled throughout these chapters are real-world case studies, like intriguing medical mysteries that offer practical lessons. These are complemented by actionable insights and applications, serving as your ethical prescription for various scenarios you might encounter in your practice.

Chapter 1: Decisiveness in Medical Ethics

'In the words of the ancients, one should make his decisions within the space of seven breaths. It is a matter of being determined and having the spirit to break through to the other side.'

It's a phrase that might make you raise an eyebrow, especially in the context of healthcare, where decisions often carry profound consequences. Are we really to make life-altering choices in the span of seven breaths? But don't be too hasty in your judgment. This ancient samurai wisdom is not a call to reckless action but an invitation to a deeper, more nuanced form of decision-making.

The Concept of "Seven Breaths"

Picture yourself as an emergency room physician, standing in the midst of a chaotic trauma bay. Multiple casualties are arriving, the medical team is looking to you for leadership, and every second counts. What's your move? You take a grounding breath, connecting you to your years of medical training, your deep understanding of triage, and the lives that hang in the balance. And then, you act. You don't just bark out orders in a frenzy; you make calculated decisions, each one a blend of instinct and wisdom. This is the essence of "Seven Breaths," a harmonious marriage between immediate action and thoughtful consideration.

Now, let's translate this ER metaphor into the broader context of healthcare. Your "trauma bay" is your realm of expertise, your "medical team" represents your healthcare staff, and the "multiple casualties" symbolize the complex ethical and medical decisions you face daily. You have a brief window of time to make choices that could significantly alter, or even save, lives. This is your "Seven Breaths" moment, a chance to prove that rapid decision-making and ethical deliberation can coexist, even flourish, under pressure.

In this high-stakes scenario, the Hagakure's principle of "Seven Breaths" serves as your ethical defibrillator, jolting you into a state of balanced urgency and understanding. It's not about making hasty decisions; it's about avoiding the paralysis that can come from overthinking in critical moments. It's about wielding your ethical defibrillator with both speed and precision, ensuring that you navigate the chaos without losing your moral direction.

You see, the Hagakure's advice to decide within the span of seven breaths is not about rushing into decisions; it's about eliminating the paralysis of overthinking. It's about cutting through the noise, the distractions, the endless 'what-ifs' that can cloud your judgment. It's about honing your focus to a razor's edge, enabling you to see the situation with crystal-clear clarity. It's like being a master archer who draws the bow with a calm mind and releases the arrow with a focused intent, hitting the bullseye not by chance but by choice.

In healthcare, this principle is not just useful; it's critical. When you're faced with a medical emergency, when the clock is ticking and the pressure is mounting, you don't have the luxury of endless deliberation. You need to act, and you need to act fast. But speed without wisdom is a runaway train, a disaster waiting to happen. That's where the "Seven Breaths" come in, grounding your actions in a bedrock of ethical deliberation, ensuring that your speed is guided by your wisdom, that your actions are anchored in your ethics.

The next time you find yourself in the eye of the healthcare storm, remember the Hagakure. Take your seven breaths— inhale wisdom, exhale action; inhale clarity, exhale decision; inhale ethics, exhale integrity. And as you take that seventh breath, let it be a breath of decision, a breath that transforms the chaos of the moment into the clarity of ethical action.

Importance in Emergency Situations

Emergency medicine can be a crucible of chaos, and a theater of the unexpected, where the line between life and death is often as thin as a scalpel's edge. It's like being a firefighter in a burning building, where every decision you make could either douse the flames or fan them, save a life or lose it. Let's delve into the adrenaline-pumping, heart-stopping world of emergency healthcare, where the principle of "Seven Breaths" transforms from a philosophical virtue into a life-saving necessity.

Picture this: the ER doors burst open, and a patient is wheeled in, teetering on the brink of life and death. The air is thick with tension, the room buzzing with the electric urgency of a ticking time bomb. You have seconds, maybe minutes, to defuse it. Extended contemplation? A leisurely debate on the ethics of medical intervention? Forget it. You might as well be asking for a cup of tea in the middle of a hurricane. This is not the time for dilly-dallying; this is the time for action, swift and decisive, yet grounded in ethical clarity.

Now, let's bring the "Seven Breaths" into this high-octane scenario. Imagine each breath as a beat of the metronome, setting the rhythm for your decision-making process. The first breath is for assessment, a rapid scan of the situation, the stakes, the options. The second breath is for prioritization, sifting through the medical and ethical variables to identify the most pressing concern. The third breath is for consultation, a quick exchange of insights and information with your healthcare team. The fourth breath is for reflection, a momentary pause to align your action with your ethics. The fifth breath is for choice, the selection of the best course of action based on the available data. The sixth breath is for commitment, the mental and emotional preparation for the chosen intervention. And the seventh breath? That's for execution, the actual implementation of your decision, the moment where thought transforms into action, where philosophy becomes practice.

In the ER, the "Seven Breaths" serve as your ethical GPS, guiding you through the maze of medical complexities with the precision of a laser-guided missile. It's not about making rash decisions; it's about making right decisions and making them right now. It's about balancing the urgency of the moment with the gravity of ethics, about harmonizing the speed of your actions with the depth of your understanding. It's like being a Formula 1 driver who knows that the secret to winning the race is not just the speed of the car but the skill of the driver, not just the power of the engine but the precision of the steering.

The Ethical Weight of Time

Think of time as the soil in a sprawling garden of medical ethics. Each decision you make is a seed planted in this soil. Some seeds need to sprout quickly, like the fast-growing herbs of emergency care. Others require more time to mature, like the slow-blooming perennials of chronic care management or medical research. The key is knowing how to tend to each seed, how to balance the need for quick growth with the need for deep roots. This is where the "Seven Breaths" come in, serving as your gardening guide, your ethical almanac, teaching you when to sow and when to reap, when to water and when to wait.

In the realm of general medicine, the ethical weight of time manifests in various ways. It could be the time-sensitive nature of a surgical intervention, where delays could lead to complications. It could be the long-term management of a chronic illness, where the ethical weight lies in the consistency and quality of care over time. It could even be in the realm of medical research, where the ethical considerations include not just the immediate impact of the study but its long-term contributions to medical science and human well-being.

The "Seven Breaths" principle encourages healthcare providers to act with a sense of balanced urgency, no matter the medical context. It's not about being hasty; it's about being timely. It's about understanding that each medical scenario has its own ethical timeline, its own rhythm of right and wrong, action and reflection. It's like being a conductor of a medical orchestra, knowing when to speed up the tempo for a dramatic crescendo and when to slow it down for a poignant adagio, always keeping the well-being of the patient as the central melody of your ethical symphony.

So, whether you're in the fast-paced world of acute care or the slow-burning realm of family practice, the "Seven Breaths" offer a universal framework for ethical decision-making. They remind you to breathe — in and out, urgency and ethics, action and reflection — creating a harmonious balance that respects both the medical and moral complexities of your practice.

Balancing Decisiveness with Informed Consent

Imagine you're a medical ethicist, standing at the crossroads of a complex case that mirrors the intricate dynamics of healthcare ethics. To your left, you have the urgency of immediate intervention, like a tourniquet ready to staunch life-threatening bleeding. To your right, you have the necessity of informed consent, akin to the carefully calibrated dosage of medication that respects the patient's physiology and wishes. Your challenge? To navigate these critical elements so that you neither compromise the patient's autonomy nor miss the window for effective treatment. It's a balancing act that requires both clinical acumen and ethical sensitivity. In the realm of general medicine, informed consent is not just a legal requirement; it's an ethical imperative, a moral covenant between the healthcare provider and the patient. It's like the foundation of a house, providing the structural integrity for the entire edifice of medical ethics. Without it, the whole thing could come crashing down, burying both provider and patient under the rubble of ethical violations and legal liabilities.

But what happens when the clock is ticking, when the sands of time are slipping through the hourglass of medical urgency? What do you do when there's no time for a detailed discussion, for a thorough review of risks and benefits, for a signed and sealed consent form? This is where the "Seven Breaths" come into play, serving as your ethical playbook, your guide through the maze of medical and moral complexities.

The principle of "Seven Breaths" teaches us to balance decisiveness with informed consent by focusing on the essence of both. The first breath is for assessment, understanding the medical urgency that demands swift action. The second breath is for communication, initiating a dialogue with the patient or their family, even if it's brief. The third breath is for transparency, providing a clear and concise explanation of the proposed intervention. The fourth breath is for listening, giving the patient or their family a chance to ask questions or voice concerns. The fifth breath is for empathy, acknowledging the emotional weight of the situation. The sixth breath is for judgment, weighing the medical needs against the ethical imperatives. And the seventh breath? That's for action, the implementation of the decision, whether it's proceeding with the intervention or pausing for further discussion.

In this ethical chess game, the "Seven Breaths" serve as your opening moves, setting the stage for a balanced and respectful interaction between decisiveness and informed consent. It's not about sacrificing one for the other; it's about finding a middle ground, a harmonious blend of medical urgency and patient autonomy. It's like being a skilled negotiator in a high-stakes diplomatic mission, knowing when to push for action and when to pause for dialogue, always keeping the well-being of both parties at the forefront of your ethical agenda.

As you find yourself caught in the tug-of-war between decisiveness and informed consent, remember the wisdom of the "Seven Breaths." Let it be your ethical choreography, guiding you through the dance steps of medical practice with the grace and poise of a seasoned performer.

The Role of Implied Consent

Obtaining informed consent can be trickier than explaining Bitcoin to your grandma. But with the Seven Breaths, you've got this! Even if the patient is unconscious, implied consent has got your back, like a solid wingman on a night out.

The concept of implied consent comes into play in situations where obtaining explicit informed consent is impractical or impossible. Think emergency scenarios, unconscious patients, or cases involving minors or individuals with impaired decision-making capacity. It's like being a lifeguard who spots someone drowning but has no time to ask for permission before diving in for the rescue. The urgency of the situation implies consent, allowing you to act in what you believe to be the person's best interest.

But let's be clear: implied consent is not a free pass to do whatever you want. It's not a blank check signed in invisible ink; it's a limited mandate, circumscribed by the principle of autonomy and the standard of reasonable care. It's like being given the keys to someone's house in case of emergency; you're allowed to enter, but only to put out a fire or feed the cat, not to snoop around or rearrange the furniture.

The "Seven Breaths" principle can guide us even here, ensuring that the use of implied consent is both ethical and respectful. The first breath is for assessment, understanding the medical urgency that justifies the use of implied consent. The second breath is for caution, recognizing the ethical boundaries that still apply. The third breath is for inference, interpreting the available clues to ascertain the patient's likely wishes. The fourth breath is for consultation, seeking input from family members or medical proxies if possible. The fifth breath is for documentation, recording the rationale for using implied consent. The sixth breath is for reflection, ensuring that your actions align with both medical necessity and ethical integrity. And the seventh breath? That's for action, the careful and considered implementation of the medical intervention.

When you find yourself in a situation where explicit consent is out of reach, remember the role of implied consent and the guidance of the "Seven Breaths." Let them be your ethical roadmap, charting a course through the complex terrain of medical decision-making, where the spoken and the unspoken, the explicit and the implicit, come together in a harmonious blend of ethical action and patient autonomy.

Decision-making Frameworks in Healthcare

Picture yourself as a surgeon, standing before an open patient on the operating table, armed with a set of surgical instruments. These instruments are your decision-making frameworks, the specialized tools that guide each incision, suture, and clamp in your ethical surgery. The "Seven Breaths" principle? That's the surgical plan, the philosophical roadmap that informs each step of the procedure. But as any seasoned surgeon knows, a plan is not enough; you need precision, technique, a set of guidelines that translate your surgical plan into life-saving actions.

In the realm of healthcare, decision-making frameworks serve as guidelines, a kind of surgical instrument for ethical operations. They're like the navigational system in laparoscopic surgery, providing real-time guidance through the intricate anatomy of medical ethics. Whether it's the Four Principles Approach, focusing on autonomy, beneficence, non-maleficence, and justice, or ethical decision-making models that incorporate cultural, social, and personal factors, these frameworks offer a structured approach to navigating the complexities of healthcare.

The "Seven Breaths" principle can be integrated into these frameworks as a foundational layer, like the sterile field upon which the surgery is performed. It serves as a reminder to breathe, to pause, to reflect, even as you follow the precise movements of your ethical navigational system. The first breath is for orientation, understanding the ethical anatomy you're navigating. The second breath is for identification, recognizing the key ethical vessels or nerves that come into play. The third breath is for evaluation, weighing these ethical considerations against each other. The fourth breath is for consultation, seeking input from your surgical team, patients, or ethical committees. The fifth breath is for deliberation, considering the potential outcomes and implications of each surgical move. The sixth breath is for decision, making a choice based on this comprehensive analysis. And the seventh breath? That's for action, the moment you make the incision, fully aligned with your ethical analysis.

In this way, the "Seven Breaths" serve as both the pre-op and post-op to the use of decision-making frameworks. They prepare the surgical field before the framework is applied, ensuring that the conditions are sterile and optimized for ethical surgery. And they close the surgical site after the framework has been applied, providing a final layer of reflection and validation, like the last suture in a well-executed operation.

Four Principles Approach and Virtue Ethics

Think of the Four Principles Approach as your vital signs—heart rate, blood pressure, respiratory rate, and temperature. These are your go-to metrics, the first things you check to get a snapshot of a patient's condition. Autonomy is like heart rate, setting the rhythm for patient-centered care. Beneficence is akin to blood pressure, a measure of how well we're enhancing patient well-being. Non-maleficence is your respiratory rate, a reminder to do no harm, to let the patient breathe easy. And justice? That's your body temperature, ensuring that resources and treatments are allocated fairly, keeping the system in homeostasis.

Now, Virtue Ethics? That's your comprehensive lab panel—the CBC, metabolic panel, lipid profile, and so on. It goes beyond the surface to examine the underlying character and virtues that should guide healthcare providers. It's like checking for markers of inflammation, electrolyte balance, or organ function. Virtue Ethics asks us to look deeper, to understand the 'why' and the 'how' behind our actions, not just the 'what.'

The "Seven Breaths" principle? I would consider it the stethoscope to use for both approaches. With each breath, you listen more closely, fine-tuning your ethical auscultation. The first breath is for orientation, understanding the ethical landscape you're navigating, much like identifying the heart or lung sounds. The second breath is for focus, zooming in on the specific ethical dilemma at hand, akin to differentiating between a systolic and a diastolic murmur. The third breath is for analysis, breaking down the dilemma into its component parts, much like you'd analyze the different lobes of the lungs during auscultation. The fourth breath is for consultation, seeking a second opinion or discussing the case with your interdisciplinary team. The fifth breath is for synthesis, bringing together your ethical 'diagnosis' and 'treatment plan.' The sixth breath is for decision, the final call on what action to take, like deciding on the appropriate medication or intervention. And the seventh breath? That's for action, the moment you administer treatment, fully aligned with your ethical analysis.

As you're navigating the complex wards of healthcare ethics, remember your ethical vital signs and lab tests—the Four Principles Approach and Virtue Ethics—fine-tuned by the stethoscope of the "Seven Breaths." Let these be your diagnostic tools and therapeutic guides, helping you provide not just clinically competent but also ethically exemplary care.

Ethical Case Study 1: The Ethical Quandary of Expedited COVID-19 Vaccines and Informed Consent

Introduction

In the annals of modern medicine, few events have shaken the world as profoundly as the COVID-19 pandemic. It's been a crisis of biblical proportions, a veritable war against an invisible enemy. In this war, the vaccines have been our most potent weapons, rolled out with a speed that's nothing short of miraculous—or is it alarming? Herein lies the crux of our ethical dilemma.

The rapid development and distribution of COVID-19 vaccines have been hailed as a triumph of science and collaboration. It's as if the global scientific community channeled the spirit of a samurai, cutting through bureaucratic red tape like a sword through silk, all in the name of saving humanity. A noble cause, no doubt, but one that raises a thorny ethical question: In our collective haste to vaccinate, have we sidestepped the sacred principle of informed consent?

Imagine being a healthcare provider in this high-stakes scenario. You're not just administering a vaccine; you're making an ethical choice that reverberates through the very fabric of society. You're caught between the urgency to act and the ethical duty to ensure that those receiving the vaccine fully understand the risks and benefits. It's a tightrope walk on a windy day, and the world is watching your every step.

This case study aims to dissect this complex ethical landscape, where the urgency of a global pandemic collides head-on with the timeless principles of medical ethics. It's a scenario that demands not just clinical acumen but ethical finesse, a situation that calls for decisiveness yet begs for caution. So, let's unsheathe our ethical swords and cut through this Gordian knot, shall we?

Background

The COVID-19 pandemic has been an unprecedented global crisis, affecting millions of lives and bringing healthcare systems to their knees. In a race against time, pharmaceutical companies, researchers, and governments collaborated in an extraordinary effort to develop vaccines. The result was a medical marvel; vaccines were developed, tested, and rolled out in record time. It was as if the entire world had mobilized like an army, with healthcare providers as the frontline soldiers and the vaccine as their primary weapon.

However, the speed of this vaccine development was both its strength and its Achilles' heel. Traditional vaccine development can take years, even decades, to ensure both efficacy and safety. In contrast, the COVID-19 vaccines were developed in a matter of months. Emergency Use Authorizations were granted, and mass vaccination campaigns were launched globally. It was a feat that seemed to echo the Hagakure's principle of making decisions "within the space of seven breaths." Swift, decisive action was taken to curb the spread of the virus and save lives.

Yet, this expedited pace came with its own set of ethical complexities. The compressed timelines for clinical trials and regulatory approvals raised questions about the thoroughness of the vetting process. Moreover, the novelty of the mRNA technology used in some vaccines added another layer of uncertainty. The public, while desperate for protection against the virus, was also wary of the breakneck speed at which these vaccines were produced.

Healthcare providers found themselves in a particularly precarious position. They were tasked with administering a vaccine that was still under Emergency Use Authorization, meaning it had not undergone the same level of scrutiny as other, more established vaccines. They were also responsible for obtaining informed consent from patients, many of whom were anxious, confused, or misinformed due to the deluge of information and misinformation circulating on social media.

In this high-pressure environment, healthcare providers had to balance the immediate, tangible benefits of vaccination— protection against a deadly virus—with the more abstract, yet equally crucial, ethical obligation to ensure informed consent. It's like being a samurai caught in a fierce battle, knowing that your actions have consequences far beyond the immediate combat. Your sword is double-edged, capable of both protecting and harming, and you must wield it with the utmost care and precision.

So here we are, at the intersection of urgency and ethics, where the lines between right and wrong blur into shades of gray. It's a complex, multi-faceted issue that defies easy answers, making it a perfect subject for ethical exploration.

Ethical Issues

The primary ethical issue at the heart of this case study is the tension between the urgency to vaccinate as many people as possible against COVID-19 and the ethical obligation to ensure informed consent. The speed at which the vaccines were developed and rolled out, while a monumental achievement, has raised concerns about whether adequate time and resources have been allocated to educate both healthcare providers and the public. This is crucial for obtaining genuinely informed consent, which is a cornerstone of ethical medical practice.

Another ethical issue is the potential compromise of vaccine safety and efficacy due to accelerated clinical trials and approvals. While the vaccines have undergone rigorous testing for emergency use, the compressed timelines naturally lead to questions about long-term effects that could only be observed in a more extended study. This creates an ethical dilemma for healthcare providers who must balance the immediate benefits of vaccination against a potentially deadly virus with the less-understood long-term risks.

Lastly, there's the issue of transparency. Given the expedited nature of vaccine development and distribution, how much information is enough to share with the public? And how does one combat misinformation in such a charged, high-stakes environment? The ethical issue here is whether withholding or inadequately communicating any information compromises the integrity of informed consent.

These ethical issues are like a set of interlocking gears, each one influencing the other. They require healthcare providers to make decisions that are not just medically sound but also ethically responsible, often within the "space of seven breaths," as the Hagakure would put it. It's a balancing act on a tightrope, with significant consequences for getting it wrong.

Stakeholders

Pharmaceutical Companies: Interested in distributing the vaccine quickly but also maintaining ethical standards.

Governments: Need to protect public health while upholding ethical principles.

General Public: Eager for a vaccine but also concerned about its safety.

Healthcare Providers: Responsible for administering the vaccine and obtaining informed consent.

Options

Here are several possible courses of action, each with its own set of pros and cons:

Continue Rapid Vaccine Distribution

Pros:

- Quick immunization of the population, potentially saving lives and hastening the end of the pandemic.
- Economic benefits as societies can reopen more quickly.

Cons:

- Thorough testing may not have been conducted due to expedited timelines, leaving questions about long-term safety and efficacy.
- Efficacy data may be skewed or incomplete, affecting the perceived reliability of the vaccine.
- The speed of the rollout could compromise the quality of informed consent, as both healthcare providers and the public may not be fully educated about the vaccine's risks and benefits.

Slow Down Vaccine Distribution for Further Study

Pros:

- Allows for more comprehensive long-term studies to assess safety and efficacy.

- Provides time to educate healthcare providers and the public, ensuring more robust informed consent.

Cons:

- Delays in vaccination could result in more COVID-19 cases and deaths.
- Economic and psychological toll as pandemic restrictions continue.

Implement a Hybrid Approach

Pros:

- Continues vaccination but at a moderated pace, allowing for ongoing data collection and public education.
- Balances the need for urgency with the ethical obligation for informed consent and safety.

Cons:

- May still not provide enough time for long-term safety and efficacy studies.
- Could create public confusion and skepticism, affecting vaccination rates.

Prioritize High-Risk Groups While Conducting Further Studies

Pros:

- Targets the most vulnerable populations for immediate protection.

- Buys time for additional research and public education on the vaccine.

Cons:

- Could be seen as discriminatory or create ethical dilemmas about who is considered "high-risk."
- Slower herd immunity, prolonging the pandemic's overall impact.

Each of these options presents a unique set of ethical challenges, requiring a nuanced approach that considers the immediate need for action against the ethical imperatives of safety, efficacy, and informed consent. It's like a samurai facing a complex battle scenario, where every move has both immediate and far-reaching consequences. The Hagakure's advice to make decisions within the "space of seven breaths" serves as a poignant reminder that decisiveness is crucial, but it must be a decisiveness rooted in ethical consideration and wisdom.

Ethical Analysis

Ah, the moment of reckoning. It's like standing at the edge of a cliff, sword in hand, sizing up your opponent. You've got your options laid out, but which one aligns with the ethical principles that guide you? Let's dissect this, shall we?

Continue Rapid Vaccine Distribution

Utilitarianism: Maximizes immediate happiness by potentially ending the pandemic sooner, but risks unforeseen negative consequences.

Deontology: Could violate the duty to ensure informed consent and long-term safety.

Virtue Ethics: Shows courage and decisiveness but may lack prudence and temperance.

Hagakure Guidance: This option embodies the Hagakure's emphasis on swift action but challenges us to consider the ethical implications.

Slow Down Vaccine Distribution for Further Study

Utilitarianism: May not maximize immediate happiness but aims for greater long-term utility through safety and efficacy.

Deontology: Aligns with the duty to provide thorough information and ensure safety.

Virtue Ethics: Exhibits prudence and temperance but may lack courage.

Hagakure Guidance: This option might align with the Hagakure's notion of thoughtful deliberation within the "space of seven breaths."

Implement a Hybrid Approach

Utilitarianism: Attempts to balance immediate and long-term utility, but effectiveness is uncertain.

Deontology: Tries to fulfill multiple duties but may fall short in each.

Virtue Ethics: Strives for a balanced set of virtues but may not fully achieve any.

Hagakure Guidance: This option presents a balanced approach but challenges us to be decisive within the "space of seven breaths."

Prioritize High-Risk Groups While Conducting Further Studies

Utilitarianism: Maximizes utility for the most vulnerable but could neglect the broader population.

Deontology: Fulfills the duty to protect the most vulnerable but raises questions about equal treatment.

Virtue Ethics: Focuses on justice and courage but could lack in universality.

Hagakure Guidance: This option could align with the Hagakure's emphasis on decisive action that considers the well-being of the vulnerable.

So, which option would a samurai choose? Which aligns most closely with the wisdom of "making decisions within the space of seven breaths"? And most importantly, which will let you sleep at night, knowing you've made the most ethical choice? Ah, the ethical battleground is a complex one, isn't it?

Recommended Course of Action

After a thorough ethical analysis, the recommended course of action would be Option 3: a hybrid approach that combines rapid vaccine distribution with ongoing, transparent research and data collection. This approach attempts to balance the urgency of the pandemic situation with the ethical imperatives of informed consent and long-term safety.

Here's why:

Alignment with Ethical Theories: This option strives to meet the criteria of multiple ethical frameworks. It aims for the utilitarian goal of maximizing overall well-being by getting vaccines out quickly but also commits to ongoing research to ensure safety, aligning with deontological duties. From a virtue ethics standpoint, it attempts to balance courage with prudence, aiming for a well-rounded virtuous action.

Hagakure Insight: The Hagakure emphasizes the need for swift yet thoughtful action. Option 3 allows for the "space of seven breaths" in its commitment to ongoing research and transparency, while also recognizing the need for decisive action in distributing the vaccine.

Stakeholder Consideration: This approach takes into account the concerns of various stakeholders. It respects the public's right to informed consent by committing to transparency and ongoing research. It also addresses the urgency that healthcare providers and policymakers feel in wanting to curb the pandemic as quickly as possible.

Mitigating Risks: While it's true that this option doesn't eliminate all risks, it does provide a framework for mitigating them. By committing to ongoing research and transparent communication, any emerging risks can be identified and addressed more swiftly than if the vaccine rollout were either rushed without sufficient data or halted for extended trials.

In essence, Option 3 offers a nuanced path that respects both the gravity and the urgency of the situation. It's a course of action that a samurai—trained to act swiftly but wisely, balancing various virtues—might choose when faced with a complex ethical dilemma. It's a path that acknowledges the weight of our choices but also the necessity to make them, and to make them well.

Conclusion

Navigating the ethical labyrinth of vaccine distribution during a global pandemic is no small feat. It's a complex, high-stakes dilemma that pits the urgency of saving lives against the ethical mandate of informed consent and long-term safety. This case study has dissected the intricate layers of this ethical conundrum, from the stakeholders involved to the ethical theories that guide our moral compass.

The recommended course of action—Option 3—stands as a testament to the nuanced, multifaceted nature of ethical decision-making in healthcare. It's not a perfect solution; no ethical decision ever is. But it's a balanced, thoughtful approach that respects the complexity of the situation. It's an approach that aims to honor both the immediate need to save lives and the long-term imperative to do no harm.

In the spirit of the Hagakure, this course of action embodies the samurai's swift yet thoughtful decisiveness. It's a choice made "within the space of seven breaths," a choice that strives to "break through to the other side" of ethical ambiguity. It's a choice that acknowledges the weight of our ethical responsibilities but also the necessity to act, and to act wisely.

As we close this chapter and reflect on the broader implications, let's remember that the principles discussed here are not confined to the realm of healthcare. They are principles that apply to the ethical dilemmas we face in our everyday lives, reminding us that the path to ethical integrity is a lifelong journey, one that requires both courage and reflection. Whether you're a healthcare provider, a policy-maker, or simply a concerned citizen, the lessons gleaned from this case study offer valuable insights into the art of ethical decision-making—a skill that, in these complex times, has never been more essential.

Chapter 2: Duty and Loyalty

'There is loyalty that protects secrets and there is loyalty that protects the truth. You must decide which is most important.'

This is a theme that has perplexed philosophers and ethicists for centuries. The Hagakure throws us into the deep end of this moral quandary, asking us to choose between two types of loyalty. It's a question that resonates deeply in the healthcare setting, where confidentiality and truth often find themselves on opposite sides of the ethical scale.

Different Types of Loyalty in Healthcare

Loyalty in healthcare is like the various systems that keep a hospital running smoothly. It's the electricity that powers the machines, the protocols that guide procedures, and the teamwork that ensures patient care. Each form of loyalty has its own specific role, contributing to the overall ethical functioning of healthcare. So, let's delve into these different roles, guided by the Hagakure's wisdom that there is a loyalty that protects secrets and another that protects the truth. Which one will you choose?

Loyalty to Patients

Being loyal to patients means respecting their autonomy, even when they make choices that have us going "Are you sure about that?" Loyalty to patients is a cornerstone in the edifice of healthcare ethics. It's not merely a procedural formality, but a deep-rooted commitment to the well-being of the person entrusted to your care. This commitment is akin to the sacred bond between a samurai and their master, as described in the Hagakure. But what does this loyalty entail in the intricate tapestry of healthcare? Let's dissect it further.

Emotions

Loyalty isn't just about medical procedures and treatment plans; it's about the emotional and psychological well-being of the patient. The Hagakure teaches us that loyalty is a complex virtue, deeply rooted in a sense of duty and compassion. When you're at the bedside, your loyalty should extend beyond the medical chart, touching the very soul of the person you're caring for. How do they feel? What are their fears? Addressing these questions is part and parcel of being loyal to your patients.

Patient Autonomy

One of the foundational principles of medical ethics is autonomy, the right of the patient to make informed decisions about their own care. Loyalty to patients means respecting this autonomy, even when it might conflict with our own medical judgment. It's about providing all the necessary information and then stepping back, allowing the patient to steer their own healthcare journey. This aligns with the Hagakure's emphasis on individual responsibility and the importance of making decisions "within the space of seven breaths."

Two other pillars of medical ethics are beneficence, the act of doing good, and non-maleficence, the principle of doing no harm. These principles remind us that our loyalty should always aim to improve the patient's condition while avoiding any actions that could cause harm. In the context of the Hagakure, this is akin to the samurai's duty to protect and serve, always with the well-being of others in mind.

Justice in healthcare means treating all patients fairly and equitably, regardless of their background, beliefs, or financial status. Our loyalty to patients demands that we uphold this principle of justice, ensuring that resources and treatments are allocated fairly. This resonates with the Hagakure's teachings on honor and the importance of serving one's community with fairness and integrity.

Healthcare is fraught with ethical dilemmas, from resource allocation to end-of-life decisions. Here, loyalty serves as your ethical compass. The Hagakure advises that true loyalty is not blind; it's guided by a strong ethical foundation. This means that your loyalty to your patient should never compromise your ethical principles. Instead, it should be a driving force that helps you navigate the murky waters of medical ethics, always with the patient's best interest at heart.

Patient Advocacy

Advocacy isn't just a buzzword; it's the heartbeat of loyalty in healthcare. It's the action you take, the voice you raise, and the stand you make for your patients. Let's break down what advocacy really means in the context of healthcare loyalty, drawing inspiration from Hagakure's teachings on active duty and unwavering commitment.

Advocacy often means questioning established norms and practices. If a treatment plan doesn't seem to align with a patient's needs or wishes, it's your duty to speak up. The Hagakure teaches us that loyalty is not about blind obedience but about a deep understanding of duty. In healthcare, this means having the courage to challenge decisions that you believe are not in the best interest of the patient.

Effective advocacy is rooted in clear, open communication. This involves not just talking but also listening—listening to your patients, their families, and even your colleagues. It's about creating a dialogue where concerns can be aired, options can be discussed, and decisions can be made collaboratively. Remember, advocacy is not a solo performance; it's a symphony of voices, each contributing to the patient's well-being.

Advocacy can sometimes put you in ethically complex situations. What do you do when the best medical option conflicts with a patient's personal beliefs? Or when resource limitations threaten to compromise patient care? Here, the Hagakure's emphasis on ethical loyalty provides a compass. It reminds us that our ultimate loyalty is to the well-being of the patient, and our advocacy should aim to navigate the best path forward, even when the waters are murky.

Advocacy doesn't stop at the hospital doors. It extends to broader issues affecting patient care, such as healthcare policies, social determinants of health, and community resources. Being an advocate may mean engaging in these larger conversations, armed with the insights and experiences you gain from direct patient care. It's about taking the principles of loyalty and duty beyond the bedside, influencing change on a systemic level.

Compassion

When we talk about loyalty in healthcare, we often start with the clinical aspects—accurate diagnoses, effective treatments, and so on. But let's dig deeper, guided by the wisdom of the

Hagakure, which teaches us that loyalty is an emotional commitment as much as it is a professional one.

Compassion is the cornerstone of this emotional loyalty. It's the ability to see the person behind the patient ID number, to understand the fears, hopes, and vulnerabilities that accompany any medical condition. The Hagakure tells us that loyalty is not just a duty but a form of deep emotional engagement. So, when you're looking at a medical chart, you're not just seeing data; you're seeing a narrative, a human story that you're a part of.

In healthcare, we have vital signs to gauge physical health. But what about emotional well-being? Compassion allows us to "measure" this less tangible but equally crucial aspect of health. It's about asking the right questions, offering a listening ear, and providing emotional support. These actions may not show up in a medical report, but they're felt deeply by the patient and can significantly impact their overall well-being.

Compassion doesn't just benefit the patient; it enriches you as a healthcare provider. It's a two-way street. When you invest emotionally in your patients, you're also reinforcing your own sense of purpose and duty. The Hagakure teaches that loyalty and duty are intertwined, and when you practice compassion, you're fulfilling your duty not just to your patient but also to yourself and your role as a healthcare provider.

Let's not sugarcoat it—healthcare can be messy. You'll encounter ethical dilemmas, resource constraints, and challenging family dynamics. In these complex situations, compassion becomes even more critical. It serves as your ethical compass, helping you navigate decisions that align with both medical best practices and the patient's holistic well-being.

Loyalty to Colleagues

Having your colleagues' backs is crucial, like a trust fall exercise at a corporate retreat. But sometimes you have to be that person who steps aside and lets them fall, if they're engaging in unethical practices. Painful but necessary, like ripping off a band aid or sitting through a mandatory HR meeting.

In healthcare, loyalty isn't just a word; it's a commitment that extends from the patient's bedside to the corridors and operating rooms where you interact with your colleagues. These are the people who share the highs and lows of your professional life, the ones who understand the unique stresses and rewards of healthcare. But what does loyalty to colleagues really mean, and how does it fit into the Hagakure's teachings on duty and discernment?

First and foremost, loyalty to colleagues is about teamwork. It's about having each other's backs in a field where the stakes are often life and death. Whether it's assisting in a complicated procedure, providing emotional support after a tough case, or simply covering a shift, this form of loyalty is what keeps the healthcare machine running smoothly. The Hagakure reminds us that there are different types of loyalty: one that protects secrets and another that protects the truth. In the realm of healthcare, your immediate community often includes your colleagues, and your loyalty to them should be rooted in truth, not just in maintaining the status quo.

However, loyalty to colleagues isn't a blank check. There will be times when this loyalty is tested, perhaps even pitted against your primary loyalty to the patient. What do you do when a colleague makes a questionable ethical decision or when you disagree on a treatment plan? The Hagakure teaches us that loyalty is not about blind allegiance but about discernment. It's about evaluating the situation and making a decision that aligns with your ethical principles and the patient's best interests. Here, the question isn't just about loyalty but about what kind of loyalty is most important: one that protects secrets or one that protects the truth?

This is where the Hagakure's teachings on the discerning nature of loyalty come into play. True loyalty sometimes means having the courage to challenge your colleagues, to question decisions, and to advocate for what you believe is right. It's not about confrontation for confrontation's sake but about striving for the greater good. This aligns with the samurai virtue of courage, which is not just physical bravery but also the moral courage to stand up for one's beliefs.

Guiding Loyalty

In these complex situations, your ethical principles serve as your guide. They help you navigate the tricky terrain of conflicting loyalties, ensuring that your actions are aligned with the best interests of the patient. This is where the Hagakure's emphasis on choosing the right kind of loyalty can be particularly useful. By focusing your mind and making a discerning decision, you can cut through the fog of uncertainty and act in a way that upholds your ethical commitments.

Loyalty to colleagues is a vital but complex aspect of healthcare ethics. It requires a nuanced approach, one that balances the need for teamwork with the ethical imperatives that guide your practice. The Hagakure offers valuable insights into this balance, teaching us that loyalty is not a one-dimensional virtue but a multifaceted commitment that requires discernment, courage, and ethical clarity. So, as you navigate the challenges of healthcare, keep these teachings in mind. Ask yourself: Is my loyalty to my colleagues enhancing or compromising my primary commitment to my patients? And most importantly, am I protecting secrets or am I protecting the truth?

Loyalty to the Institution

Institutional loyalty can be a double-edged scalpel. On one side, it allows smooth, unquestioning cuts through red tape and bureaucracy to get things done. But on the other side, it can lead to accidental self-inflicted stab wounds of ethical dilemmas if policies contradict your moral compass. Institutions rely on loyalty to maintain order, just as patients rely on you for care. But like a weary battle-scarred samurai, you must decide when to sheath the scalpel and question the established ways. It's not an easy path. But ethics before institution, like pants before shoes - that's an order you can't reverse without looking like a fool.

The Hagakure's wisdom comes into play here, reminding us that loyalty isn't a monolithic concept. It has layers, nuances, and sometimes contradictions. "There is loyalty that protects secrets and there is loyalty that protects the truth. You must decide which is most important." This quote serves as a moral compass when navigating the labyrinthine hallways of institutional loyalty.

Let's consider a scenario. Imagine your institution has a policy that prioritizes certain treatments based on financial considerations rather than medical necessity. You're faced with a decision that pits your loyalty to your institution against your ethical duty to provide the best care for your patient. What do you do?

In such situations, the Hagakure encourages us to be discerning. Your loyalty to your institution should be informed, not blind. It should be a loyalty that questions, that pushes for transparency, and that advocates for ethical integrity. It's not about causing a mutiny or being a constant contrarian; it's about ensuring that the institution itself upholds the ethical standards that justify your loyalty to it in the first place.

Moreover, this discerning loyalty may require you to take risks—whether it's questioning a superior, filing an internal report, or seeking external advice. It may put you in uncomfortable situations, where you're torn between the easier path of compliance and the rockier road of ethical integrity. But remember, as healthcare providers, our ultimate loyalty is to the well-being of our patients.

Take a moment to weigh your loyalties. Are you upholding policies that may need to be challenged, or are you being a guardian of the ethical principles that should guide all healthcare? Your actions in these moments don't just define your relationship with your institution; they define your ethical character as a healthcare provider.

The Ripple Effect of Ethical Choices

Your choices in these ethically charged situations have a ripple effect, impacting not just you and your immediate patient, but also the broader healthcare environment. When you choose to uphold ethical principles over institutional directives that you find questionable, you're sending a message. It's a message to your colleagues, to your superiors, and even to the institution itself, that ethical integrity is non-negotiable.

But let's not underestimate the challenges that come with this. Standing up for what's right in a system that may not always prioritize ethical considerations can feel like swimming against a strong current. You might face resistance, skepticism, or even repercussions. Yet, it's precisely in these moments that the Hagakure's wisdom becomes invaluable. "There is loyalty that protects secrets and there is loyalty that protects the truth. You must decide which is most important." The decision may be tough, but the path becomes clearer when you know what you're truly loyal to.

The Role of Collective Action

It's also worth noting that loyalty to your institution doesn't have to be a solitary endeavor. There's strength in numbers. If you find that an institutional policy or practice conflicts with ethical principles, chances are you're not the only one who feels this way. Collective action can be a powerful tool for change. Whether it's through formal channels like ethics committees or more informal discussions among colleagues, collective advocacy can help recalibrate the institution's ethical compass.

The Balancing Act

In the end, loyalty to your institution is a balancing act, a constant juggling of ethical principles, professional obligations, and practical realities. It's not about choosing sides but about aligning your actions with a higher ethical standard. And when the scales tip too far in one direction, when institutional loyalty threatens to overshadow ethical duty, that's when you must take a stand.

So, as you navigate the intricate corridors of healthcare, let the Hagakure guide you. Let it remind you that loyalty is not about blind allegiance but about making choices that honor not just your institution but, more importantly, the lives that you're entrusted to care for. And in doing so, you're not just being a loyal employee; you're being a guardian of the ethical principles that form the bedrock of healthcare.

Loyalty to Oneself

Self care isn't just for millennials to soak in bubble baths and post pics with #blessed. It's an ethical imperative, like staying hydrated and nourished during a grueling 14-hour surgery. You need personal fuel to keep sharp. Take care of yourself first, so you can kick ethical butt for others later. Sure, it's less glamorous than a spa facial, but getting a full night's sleep before an important procedure is critical. The hospital's sterile corridors may lack essential oils and motivational affirmations. But remember - ethical clarity comes from within, not a decorative throw pillow!

Think of loyalty to oneself as the oxygen that fuels your ethical practice. Without it, you risk ethical hypoxia—a state where poor self-care and burnout cloud your judgment and compromise your ability to make sound ethical decisions. The Hagakure reminds us that loyalty isn't just an outward expression; it's also an inward commitment. "There is loyalty that protects secrets and there is loyalty that protects the truth. You must decide which is most important." This applies to your relationship with yourself as well. Are you protecting the 'secret' of your exhaustion, or are you loyal to the 'truth' of your own well-being?

Some may argue that focusing on oneself in a field dedicated to caring for others is selfish. But let's flip that script. Self-care is not just about you; it's an ethical imperative that directly impacts the quality of care you provide. When you're mentally and emotionally drained, how can you fully engage in the complex ethical reasoning that healthcare demands? How can you be a fierce advocate for your patients if you're barely holding it together yourself?

This balance isn't just about your responsibilities to your patients, colleagues, or institution. It's also about your duty to yourself. The Hagakure teaches us that a samurai is no good to anyone if he's wounded or fatigued. Similarly, you can't serve others effectively if you're burned out, stressed, or ethically disoriented. 'Right action' in this broader sense means having the wisdom to know when to step back, when to say no, and when to prioritize your own well-being. It's about recognizing that self-care isn't selfish; it's a prerequisite for ethical practice.

The Hagakure encourages us to be introspective, to continually assess and reassess our actions and motivations. This is a crucial practice in healthcare, where the stakes are high and the ethical dilemmas are complex. Regular self-reflection allows you to identify areas where you may be falling short, not just in terms of your duties to patients and institutions, but also in your duty to yourself. Are you maintaining a healthy work-life balance? Are you taking steps to manage stress and prevent burnout? Are you continuing to learn and grow, both professionally and personally?

In healthcare, loyalty to oneself is inextricably linked with loyalty to patients and to the institution. It's a symbiotic relationship. When you're loyal to yourself, when you prioritize your own well-being, you're better equipped to navigate the ethical complexities of healthcare. You're more focused, more empathetic, and more resilient, qualities that enhance your ability to be loyal to your patients and your institution in a meaningful way.

It takes courage to prioritize yourself in a culture that often glorifies self-sacrifice. But remember, courage is another virtue highly esteemed in the Hagakure. The courage to be loyal to oneself, even when it's difficult, even when it's frowned upon, is the cornerstone of ethical practice. It's what enables you to uphold the other loyalties that define your role as a healthcare provider.

Being loyal to oneself can sometimes put you at odds with the expectations of your institution or even the immediate needs of your patients. What do you do when you're scheduled for a double shift but know that your effectiveness and ethical judgment will be compromised by fatigue? What's the right course of action when you're faced with an ethical dilemma that conflicts with your personal values? These are not easy questions, and the Hagakure doesn't offer easy answers. What it does offer is a framework for ethical discernment, a way to navigate these dilemmas without losing sight of your own well-being.

The next time you find yourself at the crossroads of an ethical dilemma, remember the ripple effect. Consider how your loyalty to yourself will reverberate through the intricate web of relationships that define healthcare. It's not just about you; it's about setting in motion a wave of ethical practice that has the power to transform your institution from the inside out.

The Hagakure and the 'Right Action'

In the labyrinthine world of healthcare ethics, the concept of 'right action' serves as a guiding light, illuminating the path of moral integrity. This principle, deeply rooted in Zen philosophy, finds its echo in the timeless teachings of the Hagakure. But what does 'right action' really mean, especially in the high-stakes, emotionally charged arena of healthcare?

Imagine you're a samurai on the battlefield of ethical dilemmas. Your armor is your training, your sword is your ethical code, and your battle cries are your principles. 'Right action' is the masterful stroke of your sword, executed with both precision and grace. It's the action that arises spontaneously, yet thoughtfully, from a state of inner balance and harmony. It's the decision that feels as natural as breathing, yet as significant as life itself.

Remember the Hagakure's lesson on 'right action.' Tune into that inner balance, that ethical equilibrium, and let it guide your hand. Whether you're deciding on a complex treatment plan or navigating a tricky interpersonal issue, that balance will help you choose the action that is not just right, but also wise. It's the way of the ethical warrior, a path that honors both the self and the other, leading to a practice that is as compassionate as it is just.

Ethical Case Study 2: The Tug-of-War: Patient Confidentiality vs. Public Health Duty

Introduction

Imagine you're walking on a tightrope, suspended high above a chasm. On one side, you have the rock-solid principle of patient confidentiality, a cornerstone of medical ethics that ensures trust and open communication between healthcare providers and patients. On the other side, you have the weighty responsibility of public health, a collective duty to safeguard the well-being of the community at large. Now, what if you find yourself in a situation where these two principles pull you in opposite directions, threatening to tip your ethical balance and send you plummeting into the abyss of moral uncertainty? Welcome to the high-stakes, real-world dilemma that Dr. Jones finds herself in.

Dr. Jones, a healthcare provider with years of experience under her belt, is faced with an ethical crisis that challenges the very core of her professional integrity. She learns that her patient, Mark, is suffering from a contagious disease that could potentially put others at risk. The catch? Mark is adamant about keeping this information confidential, invoking his right to privacy. The stage is set for an ethical showdown: a clash between the sacrosanct duty to maintain patient confidentiality and the moral imperative to protect public health.

This case study aims to dissect this complex ethical dilemma, peeling back its layers to reveal the intricate web of moral, professional, and social considerations that come into play. It's a narrative that could very well be ripped from the headlines, a situation that healthcare providers may encounter in their careers, forcing them to grapple with questions that have no easy answers. Now, let's delve into the specifics of the case and the ethical crossroads it presents.

Background

Dr. Jones is a seasoned healthcare provider, a general practitioner with over 15 years of experience. She's seen it all—from common colds to life-threatening conditions. Her reputation is one of compassion, competence, and above all, trustworthiness. She practices in a small town where everyone knows everyone, and her patients often feel more like extended family than mere entries in a medical file.

Enter Mark, a 35-year-old man who works in a local factory. He's a social butterfly, known for his weekend barbecues and active participation in community events. He's also a single father raising a teenage daughter. Mark has been Dr. Jones' patient for several years, and their relationship is built on mutual respect and trust.

Recently, Mark came to Dr. Jones with symptoms that were initially brushed off as a persistent flu. However, further tests revealed that he was suffering from a contagious disease that could pose a significant risk to others if not properly managed. The disease is not only transmissible through close contact but also has the potential to become a public health crisis if it spreads unchecked.

Here's where the plot thickens: Mark is insistent that his medical condition remains confidential. He fears the social stigma associated with his disease, the potential ostracization from his community, and the impact it might have on his job and his daughter's life. He invokes his right to patient confidentiality, putting Dr. Jones in an ethical quandary.

On one hand, Dr. Jones is bound by medical ethics and legal obligations to respect Mark's wishes. Breaking his confidentiality could result in professional repercussions and erode the trust that is so vital to the patient-provider relationship. On the other hand, she is acutely aware of the potential risks to public health. Mark's active social life and job put him in contact with many people, including vulnerable populations like the elderly and children.

Adding another layer of complexity is the small-town setting. In a close-knit community where gossip travels faster than the speed of light, news of Mark's condition could spread like wildfire, affecting not just Mark but the community's perception of Dr. Jones and the healthcare system at large.

It's a dilemma that pits two cardinal principles of healthcare against each other: the inviolable sanctity of patient confidentiality and the collective responsibility to safeguard public health. The stakes are high, the ethical landscape is murky, and the clock is ticking. Dr. Jones must make a decision, and she must make it soon.

Now, let's identify the ethical issue at the heart of this case.

Ethical Issues

The ethical dilemma in this case is a clash of titans: patient confidentiality versus public health. Both are pillars of medical ethics, but in this scenario, they're on a collision course, and Dr. Sarah is at the helm of this ethical juggernaut.

Patient Confidentiality: The cornerstone of the doctor-patient relationship is trust, and that trust is built on the assurance that personal and medical information will remain confidential. Mark has explicitly requested that his condition remain a secret, invoking his legal and ethical right to privacy. To violate this would not only potentially ruin Dr. Sarah's reputation and career but would also undermine the very essence of patient-centered care.

Public Health: On the flip side, healthcare providers have a duty to protect the well-being of the community at large. Mark's contagious disease poses a significant risk to public health, especially given his social lifestyle and work environment. Failure to act could result in an outbreak, putting countless lives at risk, including vulnerable populations.

The ethical issue is further complicated by the small-town context. In a community where everyone knows each other, the ripple effects of any decision will be magnified. What happens in the clinic doesn't stay in the clinic; it reverberates throughout families, workplaces, and social circles.

So, what is the "right" or "ethical" course of action? Should Dr. Sarah honor her commitment to patient confidentiality, thereby respecting Mark's autonomy and rights? Or should she prioritize her duty to protect public health, even if it means betraying a patient's trust?

This is not a simple case of choosing between right and wrong; it's a complex ethical puzzle where the pieces are moral principles, legal obligations, and human lives. Dr. Sarah is caught between the Scylla and Charybdis of medical ethics, and navigating these treacherous waters requires more than medical expertise—it demands ethical wisdom.

In light of the Hagakure's wisdom, "There is loyalty that protects secrets and there is loyalty that protects the truth. You must decide which is most important," Dr. Jones finds herself at a crossroads. She's caught in a tug-of-war between two loyalties: one to her patient's confidentiality and another to the well-being of the community. The ethical dilemma she faces is a ticking clock, urging her to make a decision that honors both loyalties without compromising either. It's a test of her ability to "break through to the other side," to make a choice that navigates the narrow strait between two conflicting duties.

Stakeholders

Dr. Jones: Bound by medical ethics to maintain patient confidentiality but also has a duty to public health.

Mark: The patient, who values his privacy and autonomy.

Friends, Family, Coworkers: Unaware of their potential exposure to a contagious disease.

General Public: Also at potential risk if the disease spreads.

Options

In this ethical quagmire, Dr. Sarah has several courses of action, each with its own set of pros and cons. Let's delve into these options, considering how they might affect the various stakeholders involved.

Full Disclosure to Authorities: Dr. Sarah could report Mark's condition to public health authorities, ensuring that those at risk are informed and can take preventive measures.

> **Pros**: This would likely be the most effective way to prevent the spread of the disease, fulfilling a duty to public health.

> **Cons**: It would violate patient confidentiality and could result in severe social and emotional consequences for Mark.

Confront Mark and Urge Self-Disclosure: Dr. Sarah could confront Mark about the ethical and public health implications of his secrecy, urging him to inform those at risk.

> **Pros**: This maintains some level of patient confidentiality and gives Mark the opportunity to take responsibility.
>
> **Cons**: There's no guarantee that Mark will follow through, potentially putting others at risk.

Anonymous Tip: Dr. Sarah could send an anonymous tip to Mark's close contacts, warning them to get tested for the contagious disease without revealing Mark as the source.

> **Pros**: This would protect some level of patient confidentiality while also taking steps to protect public health.
>
> **Cons**: It could create general panic or suspicion among Mark's friends, family, and coworkers.

Do Nothing: Dr. Sarah could respect patient confidentiality to the letter and take no action.

> **Pros**: This would fully honor the principle of patient confidentiality.
>
> **Cons**: It would neglect a clear public health risk, potentially leading to the spread of the disease.

Consult an Ethics Committee: Dr. Sarah could bring the dilemma to her institution's ethics committee for a collective decision.

> **Pros**: This would distribute the ethical burden and potentially lead to a more nuanced decision.
>
> **Cons**: It could delay action, allowing more time for the disease to spread.

Each of these options presents a unique set of ethical challenges and implications. Some lean more towards the protection of public health, while others prioritize patient confidentiality.

Ethical Analysis

In this intricate ethical dilemma, we can employ various ethical frameworks to dissect the options at hand. Let's delve into utilitarianism, deontology, and virtue ethics, and also draw insights from the Hagakure.

Full Disclosure to Authorities

Utilitarianism: Could maximize overall well-being by preventing disease spread but risks stigmatization and mistrust.

Deontology: Violates the duty of patient confidentiality.

Virtue Ethics: Shows courage and justice but may lack trustworthiness and integrity.

Hagakure Guidance: This option embodies swift action but challenges us to consider the ethical weight of confidentiality.

Confront Mark and Urge Self-Disclosure

Utilitarianism: Might not maximize immediate well-being but aims for long-term utility by preserving patient-doctor trust.

Deontology: Aligns with the duty to maintain patient confidentiality while mitigating harm.

Virtue Ethics: Exhibits prudence and trustworthiness but may lack courage.

Hagakure Guidance: This option aligns with the

Hagakure's notion of thoughtful deliberation within the "space of seven breaths."

Anonymous Tip

Utilitarianism: Attempts to balance immediate and long-term utility, but effectiveness is uncertain. **Deontology**: Tries to fulfill multiple duties but may fall short in each. **Virtue Ethics**: Strives for a balanced set of virtues but may not fully achieve any.

Hagakure Guidance: This option presents a balanced approach but challenges us to be decisive within the "space of seven breaths."

Do Nothing

Utilitarianism: Likely results in the least utility by allowing the disease to spread.

Deontology: Upholds the duty to patient confidentiality but neglects the duty to do no harm.

Virtue Ethics: Demonstrates loyalty but could lack in courage and justice.

Hagakure Guidance: This option could be seen as avoiding the issue rather than confronting it decisively.

Consult an Ethics Committee

Utilitarianism: Could maximize utility through collective wisdom but delays could result in more harm.

Deontology: Shares the ethical burden but doesn't absolve the individual healthcare provider of their duties.

Virtue Ethics: Shows humility and prudence but may avoid a personal ethical stance.

Hagakure Guidance: This option might align with the Hagakure's emphasis on collective wisdom but challenges us to consider the urgency of the situation.

Hagakure Insight

The Hagakure's wisdom—"There is loyalty that protects secrets and there is loyalty that protects the truth. You must decide which is most important"—serves as a guiding light. It nudges us to be both decisive and deeply considerate. Each option requires us to weigh the conflicting loyalties against the ethical principles at stake. The Hagakure would likely advocate for a course of action that harmonizes these conflicting loyalties, challenging us to find that delicate balance.

In summary, each option presents its own ethical challenges and aligns differently with various ethical theories. The Hagakure's wisdom reminds us that loyalty to secrets and loyalty to truth are not mutually exclusive but can, and should, coexist. It's akin to a samurai who must act swiftly yet thoughtfully, his every move a blend of speed and ethical precision.

Recommended Course of Action

In the labyrinth of ethical complexities, the Hagakure offers a beacon of clarity: "There is loyalty that protects secrets and there is loyalty that protects the truth. You must decide which is most important." This ancient wisdom forces us to confront the essence of our ethical dilemma: the tension between safeguarding a patient's confidentiality and protecting the well-being of the community.

So, what's the most honorable course of action? If we were to follow the Hagakure's guidance, we'd recognize that loyalty isn't a one-size-fits-all virtue. It's a nuanced concept that requires us to weigh the gravity of the secrets we keep against the potential harm they could cause. In this case, the secret — a contagious disease — poses a significant risk to public health. The truth, therefore, isn't just a matter of honesty; it's a safeguard against harm.

Given the ethical frameworks we've explored, Option 2: Confront Mark and Urge Self-Disclosure seems to strike the most balanced approach. It aligns well with deontological principles by upholding the duty to maintain patient confidentiality while also attempting to mitigate harm. From a utilitarian perspective, it could lead to greater long-term utility by preserving the patient-doctor relationship and potentially preventing the spread of the disease. In terms of virtue ethics, this option embodies prudence, courage, and trustworthiness.

But let's not forget the Hagakure's wisdom. The quote nudges us to be decisive, to make a choice that harmonizes conflicting loyalties. By confronting Mark and urging him to disclose his condition, we're not just protecting his secret; we're also protecting the truth — the truth that could save lives. We're making a decision within the "space of seven breaths," as the Hagakure would say, a decision that's both swift and ethically sound.

In essence, we're choosing a loyalty that protects not just secrets, but also the greater truth: the well-being of the community. And in doing so, we're honoring the very essence of medical ethics, the delicate balance between individual rights and collective responsibilities. It's a decision that would make any samurai proud.

Conclusion

Navigating the treacherous waters of ethical dilemmas in healthcare is no small feat. It's akin to a samurai walking a tightrope, balancing his sword in one hand and his honor in the other. In this case study, we've delved into the murky depths of conflicting loyalties and duties, exploring the tension between patient confidentiality and public health. We've grappled with the ethical issue of whether to disclose a patient's contagious disease to protect the community, a dilemma that pits the sanctity of the doctor-patient relationship against the broader responsibility to society.

We've examined this complex scenario through various ethical lenses—utilitarianism, deontology, and virtue ethics— and sought guidance from the ancient wisdom of the Hagakure. Each framework offered its own insights, its own pros and cons, but it was the Hagakure that cut through the fog, reminding us that "There is loyalty that protects secrets and there is loyalty that protects the truth. You must decide which is most important."

In the end, we recommended a course of action that honors both the individual and the community, one that respects the patient's right to confidentiality while also acknowledging the imperative to protect public health. It's a decision that embodies the Hagakure's call for decisive action, for making choices within the "space of seven breaths" that are both swift and ethically sound.

But let's not forget that this is just one case, one ethical puzzle in a field rife with moral complexities. The principles and frameworks discussed here are not just academic exercises; they're practical tools, ethical compasses that can guide healthcare providers through the labyrinth of real-world dilemmas. And beyond the realm of healthcare, these principles have broader applications in our everyday lives, reminding us that ethical decision-making is not confined to the clinic or the hospital but is a constant companion in our journey through life.

As you close this chapter and step back into the world, remember that the path of ethical practice is a lifelong journey, one that requires constant vigilance, reflection, and, yes, a bit of samurai spirit. Because, in the end, isn't that what it's all about? Being warriors of virtue, in a world that so desperately needs it.

Chapter 3: Mindfulness

'If one fully understands the present moment, there will be nothing else to do, and nothing else to pursue.'

Personally, the concept of mindfulness has always been the most elusive and challenging aspect of healthcare. It's not that I don't recognize its importance; it's that my mind is perpetually racing seven steps ahead. While some might see this as an asset, a way to anticipate challenges and prepare for the future, it often pulls me away from the here and now. I find myself mentally rehearsing for a complex process or presentation next week while I'm in the middle of a patient consultation today. The irony isn't lost on me: in a profession where every moment can carry immense weight, my tendency to leap ahead can sometimes mean missing the significance of the present. It's in the present where diagnoses are made, treatments are administered, and lives are changed. So, let's delve into why being fully present is not just a lofty ideal but a practical necessity in healthcare.

Mindfulness in Healthcare Education

Mindfulness in Healthcare Education is a topic that's gaining traction, and for good reason. The healthcare landscape is fraught with ethical challenges, and the stakes are incredibly high. So, where better to start instilling the principles of mindfulness than in the educational settings that shape our future healthcare providers? Let's delve into why this is so crucial.

Firstly, let's consider the traditional medical and nursing curricula. They're packed with rigorous courses in anatomy, pharmacology, pathology, and the like. While these subjects are undeniably important, they often leave little room for the softer skills like communication, empathy, and ethical decision-making. Yet, these are the very skills that often make the difference between a competent healthcare provider and an exceptional one. This is where mindfulness training can fill a significant gap.

By incorporating mindfulness into healthcare education, we're not just teaching future doctors and nurses how to be present; we're teaching them how to be ethically present. We're equipping them with the tools to navigate the gray areas, the complex ethical dilemmas that don't have clear-cut answers. Mindfulness training can serve as a kind of ethical simulation lab, a safe space to explore the nuanced challenges they'll face in the real world.

Now, let's talk about stress. Medical and nursing schools are notoriously stressful environments, and this stress often carries over into professional life. Mindfulness training can act as a form of early intervention, providing students with coping mechanisms that will serve them well in their high-pressure careers. It's like giving them a psychological first-aid kit that they can carry into every patient interaction, every ethical decision, every moment of doubt.

But it's not just about stress reduction; it's about clarity of thought. When you're mindful, you're better able to separate the signal from the noise. In a healthcare setting, this means being able to focus on what truly matters: the well-being of the patient. This clarity is invaluable when faced with ethical decisions that require a delicate balancing act between competing interests, such as patient autonomy versus public safety.

So, how does this tie back to Hagakure's wisdom? "If one fully understands the present moment, there will be nothing else to do, and nothing else to pursue." By training healthcare providers to be fully present from the get-go, we're setting them up to be ethical stewards of their profession. They'll be better prepared to face the inevitable challenges that come their way, grounded in a mindfulness practice that enriches not just their own lives but the lives of the patients they serve.

Mindfulness in healthcare education isn't just an elective or a 'nice-to-have.' It's a foundational skill that can shape the ethical landscape of healthcare for years to come. It's about time we make it a standard part of the curriculum.

Mindfulness in Healthcare Practice

Cultivating mindfulness improves patient interactions, no doubt. Being fully present and engaged allows deeper connections and insights. But let's get real – some days being mindful takes Herculean effort. How focused can you be when your pager is blowing up with 911s, three family members are grilling you about medications, and an orderly just spilled cold coffee down the back of your last clean white coat?

Staying mentally anchored in the chaotic reality of medicine requires ninja-level focus and Zen-master patience. Between emergency codes, lab result mix-ups, and that one co-worker who you just CAN'T with, you're lucky if you can even remember your own name and why you ever decided to go to join the profession instead of becoming a professional napper. The key is to find little pockets of sanity, like hiding out in the X-ray room or "accidentally" putting your pager through the wash. Self-care through strategic incompetence – you'll get there eventually!

Mindfulness in healthcare is far more than a buzzword or a fleeting trend; it's an essential skill that's as crucial to a healthcare provider as a stethoscope is to a cardiologist. Just as a stethoscope amplifies the sounds of the heart, allowing for accurate diagnosis and treatment, mindfulness amplifies your awareness, tuning you into the subtleties that can make a significant difference in patient care. These subtleties could be non-verbal cues from a patient, a slight inconsistency in test results, or even your own gut feelings about a diagnosis.

Being fully present isn't about merely showing up and doing your job. It's about immersing yourself in the task at hand, whether that's diagnosing an illness, planning a course of treatment, or having a difficult conversation with a patient or their family. It's the difference between simply looking at a patient's chart and truly understanding the story that the medical data is telling you.

When you're fully present, you're not on autopilot, mindlessly flipping through patient files or mechanically administering treatments. Instead, you're engaged in each moment, your mind sharp, your senses keen, and your focus unwavering. This heightened state of awareness enables you to make more accurate diagnoses, devise more effective treatment plans, and navigate the complex ethical terrain of healthcare with greater clarity and confidence. In essence, mindfulness equips you with the mental and emotional tools you need to excel in the multi-faceted, often high-stakes world of healthcare.

Reducing Medical Errors

Reducing medical errors is a top priority in healthcare, and the role of mindfulness in this context can't be overstated. When your mind is scattered or preoccupied—akin to the Zen concept of the "monkey mind"—the risk of making a mistake skyrockets. These aren't just minor oversights; they can be life-altering errors like administering the wrong dosage of medication, misinterpreting a crucial lab result, or making an incorrect incision during surgery.

Mindfulness practices act as a safeguard against these pitfalls. Think of it as a pre-operative checklist for your cognitive functions, ensuring that your mental faculties are as sterile and prepared as your surgical instruments. By engaging in mindfulness, you're essentially doing a mental deep-clean, sweeping away distractions, anxieties, and irrelevant thoughts. This heightened focus allows you to approach each task with the precision and care it deserves, significantly reducing the chance of errors. It's not just about being careful; it's about being present in your care, fully attuned to the task at hand.

The concept of reducing medical errors through mindfulness is a deep well worth exploring. In the high-stakes environment of healthcare, even the smallest lapse in attention can have catastrophic consequences. It's not just about the immediate impact, either; a single mistake can ripple through a patient's life, affecting their trust in the healthcare system and even leading to long-term complications or disability.

So, how does mindfulness act as a countermeasure to this? It's more than just a momentary pause or a deep breath. Mindfulness is a sustained practice that trains your brain to engage fully with the present, to be aware of each nuance in a patient's condition, each detail in a medical chart, and each step in a complex procedure. It's akin to tuning an instrument before a concert; the better the tuning, the more harmonious the performance.

In practical terms, mindfulness could mean double-checking a patient's medication allergies before administering a drug, even if you're rushed and even if you think you already know. It could mean taking an extra moment to confirm a surgical site, even when you're confident you're correct. It could mean actively listening to a patient's concerns instead of mentally preparing your next task. Each of these actions may seem small in isolation, but collectively, they create a safety net of attentiveness that can catch potential errors before they occur.

Moreover, mindfulness fosters a culture of accountability and continuous improvement. When you're mindful, you're more likely to reflect on your actions and decisions, to seek feedback, and to make necessary adjustments. This isn't just beneficial for you as an individual healthcare provider; it elevates the standard of care across the board.

In essence, mindfulness isn't a quick fix but a long-term strategy, a fundamental shift in how healthcare providers approach their work. It's not just about avoiding mistakes; it's about striving for excellence in every facet of patient care. And in a field where the stakes are literally life and death, can we afford not to be mindful?

Enhancing Patient-Provider Interactions

Being a mindful healthcare provider transforms the very essence of your interactions with patients. It's like the difference between a routine check-up and a comprehensive diagnostic exam; the former might catch the obvious issues, but the latter delves deeper, revealing nuances that could be critical to a patient's well-being. When you're truly present in your conversations with patients, you're not just going through the motions of asking questions and ticking off boxes. You're engaging in a meaningful dialogue that can uncover hidden fears, unspoken concerns, or even symptoms that the patient themselves might not have recognized as significant.

This heightened level of communication is invaluable in establishing trust. Patients can sense when you're fully engaged, and that attentiveness reassures them that they're in capable hands. It's akin to the comfort one feels when a skilled phlebotomist draws blood—a procedure that could be anxiety-inducing becomes a non-issue because you know you're in the hands of an expert.

Moreover, this quality of interaction is crucial when it comes to ethical considerations like informed consent. Being mindful ensures that you provide all the necessary information in a clear and understandable manner, and it also means you're more attuned to the patient's responses. You'll pick up on cues that might indicate confusion or hesitation, allowing you to address these issues on the spot. It's like reading the vital signs of the conversation, catching any abnormalities before they escalate into real problems.

And let's not forget the therapeutic value of good communication. Patients who feel heard and understood are more likely to be compliant with treatment plans, more forthcoming with information, and more proactive in their healthcare. In this way, mindfulness enhances not just the ethical quality of your care, but its effectiveness as well.

In a healthcare landscape that's increasingly complex and fraught with ethical pitfalls, can we afford not to be mindful communicators? The answer is clear: Mindfulness is not just a personal asset; it's a professional and ethical imperative.

Mindfulness and Team Dynamics

Mindfulness in Team Dynamics is a topic that often gets overshadowed by the focus on individual patient care. However, it's a crucial component of healthcare that can significantly impact both the ethical and practical aspects of medical practice. Let's dig into this.

Yes, a mindful healthcare team is the ideal. But let's get real – some people just push your buttons, no matter how "present" you try to be! Bad attitudes aren't cured by breathing exercises and vision boards. When Bob from Radiology gets snarky with you over an imaging request, the mindful response might be to let that anger radiate out of you. The natural response? Visualizing throwing that ultrasound machine at his head!

Staying Zen under pressure is tough, especially when surrounded by people who feed the flames. And while verbal flares ups won't help, allowing some mental venting can keep your cool intact. Picture polite comebacks and witty one-liners; don't actually say them out loud! With practice, you'll get better at letting irritants roll off your back, while maintaining just enough edge to stand your ground. Stay sharp, but chill!

In a healthcare setting, teamwork isn't just a nice-to-have; it's a life-or-death necessity. From the ER to the operating room, from the nursing station to the administrative offices, the ability to work cohesively as a team can dramatically affect patient outcomes. But what fuels this teamwork? What makes it effective? The answer, surprisingly, lies in the practice of mindfulness.

Being present isn't just about focusing on your tasks; it's about being aware of your surroundings, including the people you're working with. When team members are mindful, they're more attuned to each other's cues. They pick up on subtle signs of stress or confusion that might otherwise go unnoticed. They listen more carefully, not just to patients but to each other, fostering a culture of open communication and mutual respect.

Now, let's tie this back to ethics. In a high-stakes environment like healthcare, ethical dilemmas are not just individual challenges; they're team challenges. When a difficult case arises—say, a patient with complex needs that require coordinated care from multiple specialists—the team's ability to communicate openly and effectively becomes an ethical imperative. A lapse in communication could lead to a lapse in care, and that's where mindfulness comes in.

Mindfulness equips team members with the emotional intelligence to navigate these complex ethical waters. It encourages a form of collective ethical awareness, where team members not only hold themselves accountable but also feel a shared responsibility for the ethical implications of their work. This collective awareness can be a powerful tool for ethical decision-making, providing a shared framework for evaluating the risks and benefits of different courses of action.

Moreover, mindfulness fosters empathy, not just for patients but for colleagues. In a mindful team, members are more likely to consider the ethical implications of their actions on their colleagues' professional responsibilities and emotional well-being. This creates a supportive work environment where ethical practice is not just an individual burden but a collective aspiration.

When you find yourself in a team meeting or a collaborative patient care situation, take a moment to be truly present. Tune into not just what's being said, but how it's being said. Pay attention to the emotional undertones in the room. Are people stressed? Confused? Overwhelmed? Use your mindfulness skills to pick up on these cues and address them openly. Your team will be better for it, and so will your patients.

Mindfulness as an Ethical Practice

Mindfulness as an ethical cornerstone is like the Hippocratic Oath for your daily interactions—it's a commitment to do no harm, not just physically but emotionally and psychologically as well. When you're fully present, you're not just treating symptoms; you're treating the whole person. This holistic approach is the epitome of beneficence, the ethical principle that calls us to act in the best interest of the patient. It's akin to a surgeon who not only removes a tumor but also takes steps to ensure the patient's overall well-being during recovery.

Being mindful also enhances your ability to respect patient autonomy. When you're fully present, you're more attuned to the subtle cues that might indicate a patient's discomfort or hesitation. This heightened awareness allows you to address these issues immediately, ensuring that the patient's autonomy is respected at all times. It's like being a vigilant guardian of a patient's right to self-determination, always on the lookout for any threats to this fundamental ethical principle.

And let's not forget non-maleficence, the principle that calls us to do no harm. A mindful healthcare provider is less likely to make errors, whether it's in diagnosis, treatment planning, or medication administration. It's as if you have an internal safety net, catching potential mistakes before they can do harm. This is non-maleficence in action, a proactive approach to avoiding harm that goes beyond mere compliance with rules and regulations.

Mindfulness and Burnout:

Burnout is a topic that hits close to home for many healthcare providers. Burnout is like a chronic illness in the healthcare industry, eroding the quality of care and compromising ethical standards. It's a silent epidemic that often goes unnoticed until it's too late, manifesting in decreased empathy, increased errors, and a disconnection from the very principles that drew us to healthcare in the first place. So, how can mindfulness serve as a preventive measure, a vaccine if you will, against this pervasive issue?

First, let's talk about the symptoms of burnout: emotional exhaustion, depersonalization, and a reduced sense of personal accomplishment. These symptoms are not just detrimental to the healthcare provider; they're detrimental to the patient. When a provider is burned out, their ability to make ethical decisions is compromised. It's like trying to perform surgery with a blunt scalpel; you're not as effective, and the risk of harm is greater.

When you're feeling totally burned out and ready to quit medicine altogether, taking a pause to recenter through mindfulness is undoubtedly helpful. Meditate on your purpose, do some restorative yoga, and realign with your motivation to heal. But let's be honest - sometimes you need concrete steps too!

Little acts of self-preservation go a long way. Make that coffee or snack run last just a few minutes longer. Fake a bathroom break to get away from stressful situations for a moment. "Accidentally" delete the HR rep's email so you're not tempted to write them a strongly-worded resignation letter after a bad shift! Don't have the number for payroll? Even better! Out of sight, out of mind.

Staying mindful when you're running on fumes takes Jedi-level skills. But don't wait until you reach a breaking point - be proactive with mini stress relievers along the way. Your future Zen self will thank you!

By practicing mindfulness, healthcare providers can cultivate a heightened awareness of their emotional and mental state. This self-awareness acts as an early warning system, alerting them when they're veering into the danger zone of burnout. It's akin to the vital signs monitor in a patient's room, providing real-time data that can be a lifesaver when heeded.

But mindfulness does more than just sound the alarm; it offers a way out. Through mindfulness practices like meditation, deep breathing, and mindful reflection, healthcare providers can recharge their emotional batteries. It's like taking your car in for a tune-up before it breaks down on the highway. These practices help to reset the mind, clear emotional clutter, and refocus on what's important: providing ethical, compassionate care.

Now, let's connect this back to the Hagakure's wisdom: "If one fully understands the present moment, there will be nothing else to do, and nothing else to pursue." When you're burned out, you're not fully present. Your mind is elsewhere, consumed by stress, fatigue, and disillusionment. But when you're mindful, you're here, in the now, fully engaged in your work and your ethical responsibilities. You're not just going through the motions; you're living your professional oath.

Moreover, mindfulness can help healthcare providers maintain their ethical compass. When you're mindful, you're more attuned to the ethical dimensions of your actions and decisions. You're more likely to pause and consider the implications of your choices, rather than making snap judgments that you might later regret. It's like having a built-in ethical advisor, always there to guide you toward the right course of action.

Mindfulness isn't just a tool for personal well-being; it's a safeguard for ethical integrity. By incorporating mindfulness practices into our professional lives, we can fortify ourselves against the corrosive effects of burnout, ensuring that we remain ethical stewards of our noble profession.

Hagakure Wisdom

Now, how does this connect with the wisdom of the Hagakure? The teaching, "If one fully understands the present moment, there will be nothing else to do, and nothing else to pursue," serves as a profound reminder. When you're fully present, you're not distracted by what's coming next or burdened by what has passed. You're here, now, fully engaged in the task at hand. And when that task is healthcare, being fully present means you're not just doing your job; you're fulfilling a sacred ethical duty.

The wisdom of the Hagakure isn't just an ancient philosophy; it's a living, breathing guide for modern healthcare. When it says, "If one fully understands the present moment, there will be nothing else to do, and nothing else to pursue," it's not just talking about a state of Zen enlightenment. It's talking about a state of ethical enlightenment as well. Being fully present isn't just a state of mind; it's a state of being that permeates every interaction, every decision, and every action you take as a healthcare provider.

When you're fully present, you're not just ticking off tasks on a to-do list; you're deeply engaged in each task, giving it the full measure of your attention and expertise. This is what it means to fulfill a "sacred ethical duty." You're not just treating patients; you're honoring their humanity, their autonomy, and their intrinsic worth. You're not just avoiding harm;

you're actively promoting well-being. You're not just following protocols; you're embodying the highest ethical standards of your profession.

In this heightened state of awareness, mindfulness becomes the ethical lens through which you view your entire practice. It's like having an MRI for ethical dilemmas, providing a detailed, nuanced view that allows you to navigate even the most complex situations with clarity and integrity. It's not just about avoiding mistakes or preventing harm, although those are important benefits. It's about elevating your practice to a higher ethical plane, one where every action is not just correct but also compassionate, not just legal but also ethical.

And let's be clear: this isn't some optional, "nice-to-have" skill. This is foundational. Just as you wouldn't perform surgery without sterilizing the instruments, you shouldn't practice healthcare without cultivating mindfulness. It is essential. It's the underpinning of ethical practice, the "hygiene factor" that determines not just the quality of your care, but the integrity of your character.

The next time you're engulfed in the chaos of a demanding day, let this wisdom be your anchor. Pause, breathe, and ground yourself in the here and now. This isn't merely a mental timeout; it's a fine-tuning of your ethical compass, a reconnection with the foundational principles that steer your practice. In that brief oasis of mindfulness, you'll discover more than just tranquility; you'll gain the sharpness and focus required to be not just a healthcare provider, but a guiding light in the intricate, ever-evolving world of contemporary medicine.

Ethical Case Study 3: Mindfulness in Patient Care: The Ethical Dilemma of Speed vs. Quality

Introduction

In the bustling corridors of a high-stress, high-stakes urban hospital, the clock is more than just a timekeeper; it's a taskmaster, a relentless overlord that governs the lives of healthcare providers and patients alike. Here, amidst the ceaseless rhythm of life and death, we find Nick, a seasoned male nurse with over 15 years of experience. He's a man caught in the crossfire of two conflicting worlds: the institutional realm that demands speed, efficiency, and a relentless focus on metrics, and the deeply personal universe of patient care, where empathy, attentiveness, and quality are the gold standards.

Nick's daily routine is a juggling act, a balancing game of time and tasks that leaves little room for error. Each day, he faces a barrage of responsibilities—from administering medications and updating records to comforting distressed families and consulting with doctors. The hospital's ethos, driven by budget constraints and administrative pressures, is clear: Time is of the essence. Efficiency is king. Yet, Nick's own ethos, shaped by years of hands-on patient care, tells a different story. For him, each patient is a unique individual deserving of his full attention, not just another checkbox on his ever-growing to-do list.

This ethical tension forms the heart of our case study. It's a tension that Nick, like many healthcare providers, feels acutely. It's a tension that raises uncomfortable but essential questions: In the race against the clock, what gets sacrificed? Is it possible to reconcile the system's demand for speed with the moral imperative for quality care? And where does mindfulness—the art of being fully present—fit into this complex ethical landscape?

This case study dives deep into these questions, offering a nuanced exploration of the ethical implications of healthcare delivery speed versus quality. It examines the role of mindfulness as not just a coping mechanism but a transformative ethical practice. Through the lens of Nick's real-world dilemma, we'll explore how the ancient wisdom of the Hagakure can offer timeless insights into the modern challenges of healthcare ethics.

Background

Nick's hospital is a microcosm of the American healthcare system, a place where cutting-edge technology meets human vulnerability, where the quest for medical excellence is often at odds with the harsh realities of limited resources. The hospital serves a diverse population, from affluent suburbanites to low-income city dwellers. It's a Level I trauma center, which means it's always busy, always on the edge of chaos. The stakes are high, and the margin for error is razor-thin.

Nick works in the Intensive Care Unit (ICU), a high-pressure environment where life-altering decisions are made every minute. The ICU is a place of extremes—extreme illnesses, extreme treatments, and extreme emotions. It's also a place where the ethical dimensions of healthcare are magnified, where the tension between doing things quickly and doing things right is felt most acutely.

Nick is well-respected among his colleagues. He's known for his clinical skills, his ability to stay calm under pressure, and his genuine compassion for his patients. But he's also known for something else: his commitment to mindfulness. Nick practices mindfulness both in and out of the hospital. He meditates daily, takes mindful breaks during his shifts, and even leads mindfulness workshops for his colleagues. For Nick, mindfulness is more than a stress-reduction technique; it's an ethical practice, a way to be fully present for his patients and to make more thoughtful, compassionate decisions.

However, Nick's commitment to mindfulness is increasingly at odds with the hospital's culture of efficiency. The ICU is understaffed, and the nurses are stretched thin. They're expected to manage multiple critically ill patients, handle complex medical equipment, and coordinate with doctors, all while navigating a labyrinth of administrative tasks. The hospital administration, under pressure to cut costs and increase throughput, has introduced new performance metrics that prioritize speed and volume over quality and patient satisfaction.

Nick feels the squeeze. He's caught in an ethical bind, torn between the system's push for rapid task completion and his own moral compass that urges him to slow down and be present for each patient. It's a dilemma that goes beyond Nick, affecting his colleagues, his patients, and the very soul of the hospital.

This case study delves into Nick's ethical struggle, a struggle that encapsulates the broader ethical challenges facing healthcare providers in today's fast-paced, resource-strained settings. It's a struggle that forces us to confront uncomfortable questions about the kind of healthcare we want and the kind of healthcare providers we aspire to be.

Ethical Issues

At the heart of Nick's dilemma lies a fundamental ethical issue: the tension between efficiency and quality of care, between doing things quickly and doing things well. This tension manifests in several interconnected ethical challenges:

Patient-Centered Care vs. System-Centric Metrics: Nick's commitment to mindfulness aligns with the principle of patient-centered care, which prioritizes the individual needs, values, and preferences of each patient. However, the hospital's performance metrics are system-centric, focusing on throughput, cost-efficiency, and procedural compliance. How can Nick reconcile these conflicting priorities?

Duty to Patients vs. Duty to Employer: Nick has a moral and professional obligation to provide the best possible care to his patients. At the same time, he has a duty to his employer to meet performance targets and contribute to the hospital's overall efficiency. When these duties clash, which takes precedence?

Quality of Presence vs. Quantity of Tasks: Mindfulness encourages a quality of presence, a way of being fully attentive and responsive to the situation at hand. But the hospital's culture of efficiency measures success in terms of the quantity of tasks completed. Is it ethical for Nick to "slow down" in a system that rewards speed?

Moral Distress and Burnout: The ethical tension Nick experiences contributes to moral distress—a corrosive sense of being compromised, of not being able to practice according to one's ethical beliefs. Over time, this moral distress can lead to burnout, which has its own ethical implications, affecting not just Nick but also his ability to provide quality care.

Collective Ethics and Cultural Change: Nick's dilemma is not his alone; it's a symptom of a larger ethical malaise affecting the healthcare system as a whole. How can individual healthcare providers like Nick contribute to a collective shift toward a more ethical, mindful culture?

The Ethical Role of Mindfulness: Finally, the case raises questions about the role of mindfulness itself in ethical decision-making. Can mindfulness serve as an ethical tool, a way to navigate the complex, often conflicting moral landscape of healthcare? Or is it at risk of being co-opted by a system that sees it as just another "efficiency hack"?

These ethical issues are not merely academic; they have real-world implications for patient outcomes, staff well-being, and the broader healthcare ecosystem. They force us to grapple with the kind of healthcare we want to provide and receive, and they challenge us to find a path forward that honors both the practical realities and the ethical ideals of medical practice.

Stakeholders

Nick: As a healthcare provider, Nick is bound by ethical and professional standards to offer quality care to his patients. He also has a personal stake in maintaining his own well-being and job satisfaction.

Patients: They rely on Nick for attentive and quality care. Their health outcomes could be directly impacted by the level of mindfulness he brings to his work.

Nursing Colleagues: Working in the same high pressure environment, they could be influenced by the work culture Nick helps to create. Their own approach to patient care may be affected by Nick's decisions.

Hospital Administrators: Concerned with both the efficiency and quality of healthcare services, as these factors affect the hospital's reputation and financial standing.

Broader Healthcare System and Society: Interested in the balance between efficient and empathetic healthcare, as this has broader implications for public health and healthcare policy.

Options

Speed Over Quality: Nick could prioritize speed to meet administrative demands.

> *Pros*: Efficiency, less backlog, administrative approval.
> *Cons*: Risk of errors, reduced patient satisfaction, potential for burnout.

Quality Over Speed: Nick could choose to be fully present with each patient, even if it means falling behind on tasks.

> *Pros*: Higher quality of care, greater patient satisfaction, personal job satisfaction.
> *Cons*: Falling behind on tasks, potential administrative reprimands.

Ethical Analysis

Ah, the moment of reckoning. It's like standing at the edge of a cliff, sword in hand, sizing up your opponent. You've got your options laid out, but which one aligns with the ethical principles that guide you? Let's dissect this, shall we?

Prioritize Efficiency

> **Utilitarianism**: Maximizing the number of patients Nick can attend to could improve overall well-being.

However, the quality of care might suffer, diminishing overall utility.

Deontology: This option could neglect Nick's duty to provide the best possible care to each patient.

Virtue Ethics: Demonstrates virtues like responsibility and diligence but may lack in compassion and integrity.

Hagakure Guidance: This option embodies swift action but challenges us to consider the ethical weight of quality care.

Prioritize Mindfulness

Utilitarianism: Might not maximize immediate utility by limiting the number of patients Nick can see, but aims for long-term utility by improving quality of care and patient satisfaction.

Deontology: Aligns well with the duty to provide quality care to each patient, even if it means seeing fewer patients overall.

Virtue Ethics: Embodies virtues like compassion, integrity, and excellence in care.

Hagakure Guidance: This option aligns with the Hagakure's notion of thoughtful deliberation within the "space of seven breaths."

So, which option would a samurai choose? Which aligns most closely with the wisdom of "making decisions within the space of seven breaths"? And most importantly, which will let you sleep at night, knowing you've made the most ethical choice? Ah, the ethical battleground is a complex one, isn't it?

Hagakure Guidance:

The Hagakure quote, "If one fully understands the present moment, there will be nothing else to do, and nothing else to pursue," offers a unique lens. It suggests that by being fully present and mindful in each interaction, Nick is actually fulfilling his ethical duty. The "space of seven breaths" is not just about quick decision-making but about being fully present in one's decisions, thereby achieving a form of ethical purity and clarity.

Based on this multi-faceted ethical analysis, it seems that prioritizing mindfulness in patient care aligns well with deontological principles and virtue ethics, as well as the wisdom of the Hagakure. It may not maximize immediate utility, but its long-term benefits to both patients and healthcare providers make it the most ethically sound choice.

Recommended Course of Action

After a thorough ethical analysis, the recommended course of action for Nick would be to prioritize mindfulness in patient care. This recommendation is not made lightly; it's a calculated move, akin to a samurai choosing the perfect moment to unsheathe his sword.

Why mindfulness? Because it aligns most closely with deontological principles, which emphasize the duty to provide quality care to each individual patient. It also resonates with virtue ethics, embodying the virtues of compassion, integrity, and excellence in nursing practice.

But let's not forget the wisdom of the Hagakure: "If one fully understands the present moment, there will be nothing else to do, and nothing else to pursue." This ancient samurai wisdom nudges us toward a form of ethical purity achieved by being fully present in our actions. In the high-stakes, fast-paced world of healthcare, where Nick could easily be swept away by the tidal wave of tasks, the Hagakure serves as a grounding force. It reminds him that by being fully present with each patient, he's not just doing his job; he's fulfilling a higher ethical duty.

In practical terms, this might mean that Nick sees fewer patients in a day. But those he does see will receive his full attention, leading to better patient outcomes and higher levels of satisfaction. It's a win-win situation, not just for Nick and his patients, but for the healthcare system as a whole.

So, in the spirit of the Hagakure, Nick should take those seven breaths, center himself, and choose the path of mindfulness. It's not just the ethical thing to do; it's the right thing to do.

Conclusion

In this intricate case study, we've navigated the ethical waters of healthcare, guided by the wisdom of the Hagakure and the principles of modern medical ethics. We've explored the tension between the need for efficiency in a busy healthcare setting and the ethical imperative to provide mindful, quality care to each patient. We've identified the stakeholders, weighed the options, and conducted a rigorous ethical analysis.

The conclusion is clear yet profound: Mindfulness isn't just a buzzword or a luxury; it's an ethical necessity. It's the linchpin that holds together the complex machinery of healthcare ethics. By choosing to be fully present in each patient interaction, healthcare providers like Nick are not just improving the quality of care; they're elevating the entire ethical landscape of healthcare.

This isn't just about Nick or any single healthcare provider. It's about setting a precedent, about sending ripples through the pond of medical ethics. It's about acknowledging that the 'small concerns'—the individual interactions with each patient—are the building blocks of the 'great concerns' that shape healthcare systems and, ultimately, human lives.

So, as we close this chapter and this case study, let's remember the Hagakure's wisdom: "If one fully understands the present moment, there will be nothing else to do, and nothing else to pursue." In the realm of healthcare, understanding the present moment is not just an exercise in mindfulness; it's a commitment to ethical excellence. And that's a commitment worth making, seven breaths at a time.

Chapter 4: Compassion and Justice

'Compassion is a double-edged sword. Its will can separate as well as join; bring pain as well as joy.'

Compassion is a warm, fuzzy ideal we aspire to in healthcare. But left unchecked, it can send us barreling down an ethically slippery slope faster than a penguin on a waterslide. Picture yourself as a caring doctor with a suffering patient. Your heart cries out "ease their pain at all costs!" But your ethical brain warns "Whoa there, let's not break out the medical-grade morphine just yet..."

It's a balancing act between following your empathetic instincts and adhering to ethical principles. Stray too far trying to alleviate a patient's pain, and you could wind up on an episode of "Behind Bars with Dr. Feelgood." Of course, you aimed to help, but those ill-advised opioid prescriptions paved a problematic path.

So, take a breath, center yourself, and let compassion be your guide - but not your only guide. Sometimes you have to let your head lead, especially when your heart is begging you to "make it all better," ethics and legalities be damned. It's not easy, but neither is most of healthcare. Just ask the poor interns surviving on energy drinks and spite.

That's the double-edged nature of compassion. On one side, it's the healer, the part of us that connects on a profoundly human level. It's the voice that says, "Act now, ease suffering, make it better." But on the flip side, it can be the rogue agent, the maverick that urges us to act in ways that feel right but may not stand up to ethical scrutiny. It can lead us down paths that, while paved with good intentions, don't necessarily serve the greater good or align with the principles of justice and fairness.

If you feel that tug of compassion urging you to act, take a moment. Consider the other edge of that sword. Ask yourself: Is this act of compassion in harmony with the broader ethical landscape, or is it creating a dissonance that needs to be addressed? It's not about quashing your compassionate instincts; it's about understanding that compassion, like any powerful tool, must be wielded with both precision and awareness of its broader impact.

The Ethical Dilemmas

What do you do when two patients have an equal claim to a limited resource? Or when following the guidelines to the letter would result in an outcome that feels morally wrong? These are the ethical quagmires that healthcare providers often find themselves in, and they require a nuanced approach. It's like a samurai finding himself surrounded, forced to make a decision that will inevitably leave one flank exposed. There's no easy answer, but the principles of justice and fairness must always be your guiding stars.

Ah, ethical dilemmas. Navigating between competing principles makes juggling chainsaws seem easy. Two patients, one life-saving ventilator - what now? Do you flip a coin? Play rock, paper, scissors? Initiate a high-stakes dance battle? Or do you just curl up under your desk and hope the cruel quandary resolves itself while you hug your knees in the fetal position?

But in all seriousness, balancing acts like resource allocation in a pandemic call for a clear head and even clearer ethical principles to guide the way. When caught in a moral maze with no neat solution, seek wisdom from ethics committees, utilize frameworks cautiously, and know that you'll likely never feel 100% at peace with such wrenching decisions. Do your best and then take care of YOU. The weight is heavy, but you aren't meant to carry it alone.

Justice is a term that often conjures images of courtrooms, gavels, and legal codes. But in healthcare, justice takes on a more nuanced form. It's not just about following the law; it's about ensuring that everyone—regardless of age, race, or economic status—has equitable access to quality care. So, how does this concept of justice manifest in the complex, resource-strapped world of healthcare? Let's dive in, shall we?

The Principle of Distributive Justice

In this context, distributive justice becomes a complex ethical calculus. You're not just adding and subtracting; you're solving ethical equations with multiple variables—severity of condition, likelihood of recovery, age, and sometimes even social factors. It's like a samurai sizing up his opponents, assessing their strengths and weaknesses before choosing his target. You have to consider both immediate and long-term outcomes, balancing the urgency of the situation with the broader ethical implications.

The Principles at Play

The principles guiding this form of justice often include equity, equality, and need. Equity ensures that those who are worse off receive more attention, leveling the playing field. Equality aims for an even distribution, treating everyone as equals. Need focuses on providing resources to those who require them most urgently. It's like a samurai choosing to first take down the most dangerous enemy on the battlefield, knowing that doing so will have the greatest impact on the fight's outcome.

The Ethical Guidelines

Several ethical frameworks guide this process. The four principles of medical ethics—autonomy, beneficence, non-maleficence, and justice—serve as the cornerstones. But within the realm of justice, specific guidelines like "first-come, first-served," "sickest first," or "greatest good for the greatest number" can be applied. Each has its merits and drawbacks, and the challenge lies in choosing the most appropriate one for the situation at hand. It's akin to a samurai choosing the right technique for the battle he's facing.

Institutional Justice

Ah, institutional policies—the rulebooks that healthcare providers often lean on when navigating the labyrinthine corridors of ethical dilemmas. These policies are like the samurai's code of Bushido, offering a set of guidelines that aim to ensure justice and fairness. But let's dig deeper, shall we?

Institutional policies are essential. They're the framework that holds the ethical edifice together, providing a standardized approach to complex issues like organ transplantation, end-of-life care, and resource allocation during crises. Think of them as the katana in a samurai's arsenal—sharp, precise, and effective when used correctly.

However, these policies are not without their limitations. They can be rigid, designed to apply to the majority of situations but not all. In the same way that a samurai's katana is not the right weapon for every battle, institutional policies may not be the perfect fit for every ethical dilemma. For instance, a strict "first-come, first-served" policy might fail to consider the severity of a patient's condition, while a "sickest first" approach could overlook other factors like age or quality of life.

Then there are the gray areas, the situations that the rulebook doesn't cover. What do you do when a patient doesn't fit neatly into any category? Or when following the policy to the letter would result in an outcome that feels ethically wrong? It's in these moments that the wisdom of the Hagakure comes into play, reminding us that true mastery requires not just adherence to the rules but also the discernment to know when to bend them.

The Need for Flexibility

This is where the concept of "ethical flexibility" comes into play. Just as a samurai must adapt his techniques to the opponent he's facing, healthcare providers must be able to adapt institutional policies to the unique ethical challenges they encounter. This doesn't mean throwing the rulebook out the window but rather interpreting it in a way that aligns with the overarching principles of justice and fairness.

The Role of Ethics Committees

Many healthcare institutions have ethical committees that serve as the arbiters in complex or ambiguous cases. Think of them as the council of wise samurai, seasoned warriors who can offer guidance when the path is unclear. Their role is to interpret the policies, consider the unique aspects of each case, and provide recommendations that uphold the principles of justice.

The Social Determinants of Health

Justice in healthcare also extends to addressing the social determinants of health, such as poverty, education, and access to healthcare. It's not just about treating the symptoms but also addressing the root causes. The Hagakure would remind us that a samurai doesn't just wield a sword; he also cultivates his mind and spirit. Similarly, a just healthcare system aims to create an environment where everyone has an equal opportunity to be healthy.

The Ethical Dilemmas

Justice is not without its ethical dilemmas. What do you do when two patients need the same resource but only one can have it? How do you decide who gets priority? These are the moments when the teachings of the Hagakure come to the fore, reminding us that in matters of great concern, a balanced, mindful approach is crucial.

In essence, justice in healthcare is a dynamic, multifaceted concept that goes beyond legalities. It's about creating a system that is fair, equitable, and responsive to the needs of all patients. And like the samurai who continually hones his skills and understanding, those of us in healthcare must continually strive to ensure that our actions and decisions are just.

The Scales of Justice

Justice is like the seasoned judge in the courtroom of healthcare ethics, always asking the hard questions. "Is this fair?" "Who else is affected?" "What precedent does this set?" It's the balancing scale that doesn't waver under the weight of emotional pleas or compelling individual stories. Justice is that unwavering voice that reminds us to zoom out, to consider the bigger picture, the collective good. It's the principle that nudges us to distribute limited resources equitably, to apply rules consistently, and to treat every patient with the same level of care and dignity.

But here's the rub: Can this unwavering commitment to fairness and equality make us lose our humanity? Can it turn us into ethical automatons, crunching numbers and ticking boxes, but missing the nuanced human experience that each patient brings into our care? Imagine a scenario where two patients need a life-saving treatment, but there's only enough for one. The protocol might dictate that the younger patient or the one with a better prognosis should receive it. Justice served, case closed? Let's reflect for a moment... what about the emotional toll, the gut-wrenching feeling of having to look the other patient in the eye and say, "I'm sorry, we did the math, and you didn't make the cut"?

This is where the tension between compassion and justice really comes into play. Justice aims for the equitable, the fair, the universally applicable. It's the cornerstone of public health policies, of triage protocols, of organ donation lists. But it's also a principle that, if applied too rigidly, can make us lose sight of the individual stories, the unique circumstances that don't fit neatly into our ethical algorithms.

So, what's the solution? How do we reconcile the warm, intuitive pull of compassion with the cold, rational logic of justice? It's not about choosing one over the other; it's about finding a harmonious middle ground. It's about understanding that both are essential voices in the ethical dialogue, each checking the other's excesses. Compassion without justice can lead to favoritism, to emotionally charged decisions that don't stand up to ethical scrutiny. Justice without compassion can lead to a mechanical, dehumanized healthcare system that sees patients as numbers rather than people.

The key is to let these two principles dance together, each leading at times, but always in step. When faced with an ethical dilemma, let compassion be your initial guide, pulling you toward the human element, the individual story. Then let justice step in, asking the tough questions, providing the ethical framework that ensures your compassionate act serves not just the individual, but the collective good. It's a delicate balance, but one that's essential for ethical healthcare practice.

Ethical Pitfalls

Navigating the ethical terrain of healthcare is a bit like walking a tightrope. On one side, you have the warm, empathetic pull of compassion; on the other, the stern, equitable demands of justice. The challenge is to walk that line without tipping too far in either direction. But let's be honest: it's easier said than done. Even the most seasoned healthcare providers can stumble into ethical pitfalls when trying to balance these two principles. So, what are some of these common mistakes, and how can we sidestep them?

Overstepping Boundaries in the Name of Compassion

It's a scenario that's all too common. You're so moved by a patient's suffering that you go above and beyond to alleviate it, perhaps even bending the rules a bit. While the intention is noble, the action can sometimes lead to ethical complications. For example, administering additional medication to ease a patient's pain might seem compassionate but could risk overdose or conflict with other treatments. The Hagakure would remind us that even well-intended actions can lead to harmful outcomes if not carefully considered.

The Tyranny of Fairness

Justice is essential in healthcare, but left unchecked, its scales can tip from equitable to oppressive quicker than you can say "actuarial chart."

Sure, fairness feels noble when you're divvying up coveted Jello cups in the cafeteria line. But in life-or-death scenarios, blind justice can seem downright cold. "Only one dose left and two dying patients? Okay, medical Hunger Games it is! May the odds be ever in your favor."

While impartiality principles seem pragmatic on paper, their application can feel absurdly callous in practice. Strict "first come, first served" rationale cares little whether it's an eager foodie or a famished soul awaiting their fate in line. Discernment between lives well-lived and lives cut tragically short gets blurred in the name of "fairness."

Of course, equitable distribution protocols exist for good reason. Resources are finite, and ethical framework provides guardrails when emotion threatens to steer decisions off course. But avoid justice so unyielding that your clinic feels like a Dickensian orphanage. Temper statutes with empathy, and let compassion give cold impartiality a much-needed hug now and then.

The Savior Complex

Beware the siren call of the savior complex, luring even the most well-intentioned healers against the rocky shores of ethical pitfalls. Sure, it starts out with noble goals - go above and beyond for your patients! But soon you're knee-deep in paternalistic behaviors that strip away patient autonomy faster than you can say "doctor knows best!"

Don't let compassion morph into thinking only YOU hold the keys to a patient's salvation. Avoid tropes like showing up at their door with chicken soup or throwing out perfectly good eastern medicine for your own experimental treatments. You are but a mere mortal healthcare provider, not the lone prophet who shall lead the people to wellness.

Of course, offer your expertise humbly while respecting patient wishes. But don't let your compassion blind you to the fact that they ultimately pilot their own healthcare journeys. You're there to co-navigate, not override free will! So steer clear of the messiah mindset, lest you wind up on an ethical island talking to volleyball patients you've mandated stay under your care. Not a good look for anyone.

The Bureaucratic Trap

Rigidly adhering to policies and protocols can suck you into a bureaucratic vortex faster than a Florida retiree heads for the early bird buffet. You know the type - rule-abiding to a fault, terrified of anything outside the handbook posted online (which no one has ever read cover to cover, let's be real).

Don't become that rigid doctor who sees patients as widgetized billing codes rather than complex human beings!

Even the most procedural samurai knew that true mastery requires some wiggle room. Of course, healthcare policies exist for good reason - you can't have docs freestyling treatments like experimental DJs. But leave space to incorporate the human element into the equation.

Yes, check your liability coverage first, but don't let it turn your clinic into a creativity-crushing institution of sadness. Find ways to express your compassion within the ethical lines. Maybe it's spending a few extra minutes listening to a patient's concerns or exploring lower-cost medication options. Small things can make a big difference, even if they don't fit as neatly into the institutional spreadsheet. Spreadsheets don't have hearts, but you do!

Avoiding the Pitfalls

Navigating the swirling vortex between compassion and justice requires Jedi-level mindfulness, not just to avoid pitfalls but to leap over them like a caped crusader.

When emotions run high, take a breath and get centered, lest you find yourself on the wrong end of a malpractice suit. Regular ethical training keeps your moral compass calibrated, so you don't end up wildly off course. And discuss complex cases with colleagues to crowdsource insights, since one doctor's "of course!" is another's "absolutely not!"

The Hagakure teaches us to understand each moment in its unique context before blazing ahead. You would not blindly perform surgery; likewise, do not blindly execute ethics without reflection. Pause, breathe, consider from all angles.

This balancing act is not a one-and-done task, but a continuous tightrope walk. You will wobble, slip, even face-plant at times. But with mindful effort you will also find moments of clarity, of ethical flow, where compassion and justice dance in perfect harmony like Fred and Ginger.

Stay centered even when waves of emotion threaten to capsize your ethical ship. And don't forget to pack an ethical life preserver in case you do end up overboard! No one said this would be easy, but integrity demands work. Now let's get to it!

The Hagakure's Wisdom

The Hagakure teaches us that true mastery lies in the balance, in the ability to navigate between extremes to find the ethical "middle way." In the realm of distributive justice, this means finding a balance between the individual and the collective, between compassion and fairness, between the urgent and the important.

As you inevitably find yourself in the ethical crucible of resource allocation, remember the wisdom of the samurai. Take a moment to weigh your options carefully, to consider not just the immediate needs but also the broader ethical landscape. Your decisions may not please everyone, but if they're guided by the principles of justice and fairness, you'll know you've done your best. And in the complex, ever-changing world of healthcare, that's all any of us can strive for.

Striking the Balance

In traditional Chinese philosophy, the concept of Yin and Yang describes how seemingly opposite or contrary forces may actually be complementary, interconnected, and interdependent. This concept has been widely adopted in various forms of Eastern thought, including Japanese philosophy. Imagine compassion as the Yin, the softer, nurturing aspect that allows us to connect emotionally with our patients. Now, picture justice as the Yang, the stronger, rational force that ensures fairness and equality. Both are necessary, both are vital, but they can also be in tension with each other.

Lean too much into Yin, into compassion, and you risk making decisions based on emotional impulses. You might prioritize a patient whose story resonates with you, but what about the others who are equally deserving of care? What about the ethical principle of justice that calls for equitable treatment for all?

Conversely, if you lean too much into Yang, into justice, you might find yourself in a position where you're allocating resources strictly by the book, without considering the unique circumstances of each individual. You might uphold the principle of fairness, but at the expense of the human touch, the emotional connection that makes healthcare more than just a transaction.

So, how do you find the balance? How do you integrate both Yin and Yang into your ethical decision-making? It's like the art of Japanese swordsmanship, Kendo, where the goal is not just to strike, but to strike with a balance of strength and flexibility. You need to be firm but not rigid, soft but not yielding. It's a delicate balance, one that requires constant attention and adjustment.

In the realm of healthcare ethics, this means being aware of both your emotional responses and your ethical principles. It means asking yourself tough questions: Am I letting my emotions cloud my judgment? Am I sticking too rigidly to rules at the expense of individual needs? And most importantly, how can I ensure that my actions are both compassionate and just?

The Japanese concept of "Hara," or the body's energy center located in the belly, teaches us to act from a place of balance. It's from this center that martial artists draw their strength, and it's from this center that we too can find our ethical balance. When faced with a difficult decision, take a moment to center yourself. Feel the pull of both compassion and justice, and strive to act from a place where both are honored.

In doing so, you're not just making a decision; you're embodying the harmonious integration of Yin and Yang, of compassion and justice. And that's not just good ethics; it's good healthcare.

Ethical *Case Study* 4: Unvaccinated Children in a Vaccinated-Only Healthcare Practice

Introduction

In the fast-paced, high-stakes world of healthcare, ethical dilemmas often present themselves when we least expect them, much like sudden crossroads on a long journey. One such crossroads is the focus of this case study—a healthcare professional working in a practice with a strict vaccination policy encounters an unvaccinated child in need of immediate medical care and routine screening. The situation is further complicated by the child's socioeconomic background and the parents' personal beliefs against vaccination.

This isn't just a medical decision; it's an ethical quandary, a moral puzzle that needs solving. It's like being a samurai on the battlefield, sword drawn, facing an opponent you don't want to fight but must. Do you adhere strictly to the practice's policy, thereby protecting the collective herd immunity? Or do you make an exception, guided by compassion for a child who has no say in their vaccination status?

It's a dilemma that tests the very core of medical ethics, forcing the healthcare professional to weigh the principles of justice, compassion, and professional duty. And it's a decision that must be made swiftly, yet thoughtfully, as lives hang in the balance. Welcome to the ethical labyrinth of modern healthcare, where each choice can lead you down a different path, and the "right" way is often not as clear as we'd like it to be.

Background

The healthcare practice in question is a well-regarded institution, known for its high standards of care and strict adherence to medical guidelines. The policy on vaccinations is clear-cut: all patients must be vaccinated to receive care. This policy is in place not just as a matter of public health but also as a safeguard against potential outbreaks of vaccine-preventable diseases. It's a rule that has been communicated clearly to all staff and is generally accepted without question.

Enter the child, a seven-year-old with a persistent cough, accompanied by parents who are staunchly against vaccinations due to personal beliefs. The family is from a low-income background, and access to healthcare has been a challenge for them. They've come to this practice out of desperation; other healthcare providers in their network have turned them away due to the child's unvaccinated status.

The healthcare professional who encounters this family is seasoned, with years of experience but is also a stickler for rules. They believe in the importance of vaccinations and herd immunity, and they've seen firsthand the consequences of vaccine-preventable diseases. However, they're also deeply compassionate and have dedicated their career to helping those in need, particularly marginalized communities.

The clock is ticking. The child needs medical attention, and routine screenings that could detect other potential health issues are also on the line. But treating the child would mean breaking a cardinal rule of the practice, potentially putting other patients at risk and setting a precedent that could undermine the vaccination policy.

It's as if our healthcare professional is a samurai caught in a dilemma of duty and compassion. Do they uphold the code of their "clan," adhering strictly to the practice's policy, or do they follow their inner moral compass, making an exception for a child in need? The stakes are high, the ethical landscape is murky, and there's no easy way out. Welcome to a day in the life of healthcare, where the dilemmas are as complex as they are consequential.

Ethical Issues

The ethical dilemma here is a tangle of conflicting moral principles and competing interests. On one side, there's the principle of justice, which demands that rules and policies be applied consistently to all patients. The vaccination policy is in place for a reason: to protect the collective health of the community and prevent outbreaks of vaccine-preventable diseases. Making an exception could compromise this collective good and set a precedent that undermines the integrity of the healthcare practice's policies.

On the flip side, there's the principle of compassion, which calls for individualized care and attention to the unique circumstances of each patient. The child in question is not responsible for their unvaccinated status; that decision was made by their parents. Denying care to the child could exacerbate their health issues and perpetuate a cycle of healthcare inequality. It's a classic case of the individual versus the collective, a tension that healthcare professionals often find themselves navigating.

But wait, there's more. What about the principle of autonomy? The parents have made a conscious choice not to vaccinate their child based on their personal beliefs. While many might disagree with this choice, it's a choice they've made nonetheless. Should their autonomy be respected, even if it conflicts with public health guidelines?

And let's not forget the healthcare professional's own moral integrity. They've dedicated their life to helping others, particularly those who are marginalized or disadvantaged. Turning away a child in need would conflict with their own ethical principles, creating a moral dissonance that's hard to reconcile.

So, what's the "right" course of action? Is there even a "right" course of action? It's like being a samurai on a battlefield, caught between loyalty to your clan and the dictates of your own moral compass. The ethical terrain is fraught, the path ahead unclear. And yet, a decision must be made.

Stakeholders

The Child: The most vulnerable of all stakeholders, unable to make decisions for themselves. Their health and well-being are directly at stake. They're like a young samurai apprentice, dependent on the wisdom and choices of their elders.

The Parents: The decision-makers, the ones who chose not to vaccinate. Their motivations could range from deeply held beliefs to misinformation. They're akin to the clan leaders in a samurai tale, making choices that affect the whole family, for better or worse.

The Healthcare Professional: Our protagonist, caught in an ethical quagmire. They have a duty to uphold the practice's policies but also a personal and professional commitment to provide care. Imagine them as the seasoned samurai, skilled yet torn between duty and personal honor.

The Medical Practice: Represented by its policies and perhaps its administrative staff, this entity has a stake in maintaining a safe environment for all patients. Think of it as the fortress that the samurai is sworn to protect; its walls must remain impenetrable.

The Broader Community: Ah yes, the often-overlooked players. Other patients could be at risk if an unvaccinated child is allowed into a practice, especially those who are immunocompromised. In our samurai analogy, they're the villagers who rely on the samurai for protection.

Public Health Authorities: The overarching organizations that set vaccination policies. They're like the shogunate, setting laws and guidelines that local clans (or in our case, medical practices) are expected to follow.

The Healthcare Professional's Peers: Other doctors, nurses, and medical staff who may be influenced by the decision made in this case. They're the fellow samurai who look to our protagonist for cues on how to act and what to value.

Options

Ah, the crossroads. Every samurai knows that moment when the path diverges, and each route promises its own set of challenges and rewards. So, what are our options here?

Strictly Follow Policy: The healthcare professional could choose to adhere strictly to the practice's policy, denying care to the unvaccinated child.

> **Pros:** Upholds the practice's guidelines, potentially protecting other patients from the risk of infection.

> **Cons:** Denies necessary medical care to a child who has no say in their vaccination status and could be seen as a form of medical discrimination.

Provide Care with Precautions: The healthcare professional could opt to treat the child but take extra precautions, like isolating them from other patients.

> **Pros:** Balances the duty to provide care with the need to protect other patients.

Cons: Could be logistically challenging and still poses some risk of infection to others.

Refer to Another Facility: The healthcare professional could refer the child to another medical facility that doesn't have a strict vaccination policy.

> **Pros:** The child receives care, and the practice's policy is upheld.

> **Cons:** This could be seen as passing the buck and doesn't address the systemic issue.

Seek Policy Exception: The healthcare professional could appeal to the practice's administrative body for an exception to the policy.

> **Pros:** Could provide a more nuanced approach to care in exceptional circumstances.

> **Cons:** Time-consuming and may not be successful.

Civil Disobedience: The healthcare professional could choose to openly defy the practice's policy, accepting any repercussions in order to provide care.

> **Pros:** Makes a strong ethical stand, potentially sparking a broader conversation about the policy.

> **Cons:** Risks professional censure and could undermine the practice's policy.

Educate and Reevaluate: The healthcare professional could take the opportunity to educate the parents about the importance of vaccination and then reevaluate the situation.

Pros: Addresses the root issue and could lead to the child being vaccinated.

Cons: Time-consuming and may not change the parents' minds.

Each option is like a different battle tactic, each with its own potential for victory or defeat. And just like a samurai must consider the terrain, the enemy's skill, and the welfare of his troops, so must the healthcare professional consider the ethical implications, the potential risks, and the impact on all stakeholders. Ah, the art of ethical war!

Ethical Analysis:

Ah, the moment of reckoning. It's like standing at the edge of a cliff, sword in hand, sizing up your opponent. You've got your options laid out, but which one aligns with the ethical principles that guide you? Let's dissect this, shall we?

Strictly Follow Policy

Utilitarianism: This option aims to maximize overall well-being by protecting the majority of patients from potential infection. However, it fails to consider the well-being of the unvaccinated child.

Deontology: From a duty-based perspective, this option upholds the healthcare provider's duty to adhere to practice policies but neglects the duty to provide care to all.

Virtue Ethics: This option may lack the virtues of compassion and justice, focusing instead on rigid rule-following.

Hagakure Guidance: "Seven breaths" here might mean sticking to established rules without overthinking, but it could lack compassion.

Provide Care with Precautions

Utilitarianism: This option tries to balance the well-being of all parties involved, making it a strong utilitarian choice.

Deontology: Upholds the duty to provide care while also attempting to minimize harm to others.

Virtue Ethics: Demonstrates prudence, responsibility, and compassion.

Hagakure Guidance: This option embodies the spirit of breaking through to the other side, taking a balanced approach within the space of "seven breaths."

Refer to Another Facility

Utilitarianism: May solve the immediate issue but doesn't address the systemic problem, making it a short-term utilitarian solution.

Deontology: Fulfills the duty to the practice's policy but could be seen as neglecting the duty to the child.

Virtue Ethics: Could be seen as lacking in courage and responsibility.

Hagakure Guidance: This might be seen as avoiding the issue rather than confronting it decisively.

Seek Policy Exception

> **Utilitarianism:** Aims for a long-term solution that could benefit future patients as well.
>
> **Deontology:** Tries to reconcile conflicting duties.
>
> Virtue Ethics: Demonstrates wisdom, courage, and justice.
>
> **Hagakure Guidance:** This is a thoughtful approach, but could it be done within "seven breaths"?

Civil Disobedience

> **Utilitarianism:** Risks causing harm in the short term for potential long-term benefit.
>
> **Deontology:** Clearly violates the duty to adhere to practice policies.
>
> **Virtue Ethics:** Embodies courage and perhaps a sense of justice but lacks prudence.
>
> **Hagakure Guidance:** This is the ultimate "breaking through to the other side," but at what cost?

Educate and Reevaluate

> **Utilitarianism:** Aims to solve the root issue, benefiting both the child and society.
>
> **Deontology:** Upholds the duty to educate and provide care.
>
> **Virtue Ethics:** Demonstrates wisdom, patience, and compassion.

Hagakure Guidance: This option takes time but could be the most compassionate choice, aligning with the Hagakure's notion of a "double-edged sword."

So, which option would a samurai choose? Which aligns most closely with the wisdom of "making decisions within the space of seven breaths"? And most importantly, which will let you sleep at night, knowing you've made the most ethical choice? Ah, the ethical battleground is a complex one, isn't it?

Recommended Course of Action

Alright, let's cut to the chase. You've weighed your options, you've consulted the ethical oracles, and now it's time to make your move. It's like that moment when a samurai draws his sword, fully committed to the action that follows. There's no turning back.

After a thorough ethical analysis, the recommended course of action is to **Provide Care with Precautions**.

1. **Alignment with Ethical Theories**: This option seems to be the golden mean, striking a balance among utilitarianism, deontology, and virtue ethics. It maximizes well-being, upholds professional duties, and embodies virtues like compassion and prudence.

2. **Hagakure Guidance**: The Hagakure tells us to make decisions within the space of "seven breaths," emphasizing the need for swift yet thoughtful action. This option allows for that. It's a decisive move that also embodies compassion, aligning well with the

Hagakure's notion that compassion is a "double-edged sword."

3. **Stakeholder Impact**: This option takes into account the well-being of all stakeholders involved—the child, the healthcare team, and other patients. It aims to minimize harm while maximizing benefit, a utilitarian dream come true.

4. **Practicality**: Let's face it, we're not just dealing with ethical theories here; we're dealing with real-world implications. This option is also practical and feasible, not requiring a complete overhaul of the system or putting undue burden on healthcare providers.

5. **Long-term Implications**: This isn't just about solving an immediate problem; it's about setting a precedent for future ethical dilemmas. By choosing this path, you're contributing to a culture of ethical mindfulness and compassionate care.

So, there you have it. It's not an easy decision, but who said ethics was a walk in the park? The key is to act with both urgency and understanding, to be as swift as a samurai but as thoughtful as a monk. And remember, the ethical journey doesn't end here; it's a lifelong path, a continuous cycle of action and reflection. So, take a deep breath, make your decision, and prepare for the next challenge. Because in healthcare, there's always a next challenge.

Conclusion

This case study serves as a microcosm of the ethical challenges that healthcare professionals face every day. It's not just about making the "right" decision; it's about understanding the ethical landscape, recognizing the stakes, and acting with both courage and care. It's about being an ethical warrior in the healthcare arena, armed with the double-edged sword of compassion and justice.

And let's not forget the Hagakure's wisdom, which has been our guiding light through this ethical fog. "Compassion is a double-edged sword. Its will can separate as well as join; bring pain as well as joy." It reminds us that ethical decisions are rarely black and white; they exist in shades of gray, in the complex interplay of human emotions, duties, and societal norms.

So, as you step out of this chapter's ethical dojo, remember that the journey is far from over. Each day brings new challenges, new ethical puzzles to solve. But armed with the principles and tools we've discussed, you're well-equipped to face whatever comes your way. And who knows, maybe one day you'll look back at this case as a defining moment in your ethical journey, a stepping stone on your path to becoming the ethical clinician you aspire to be.

Chapter 5: Honor and Integrity

'To give a person one's opinion and correct his faults is an important thing. It is compassionate and comes first in matters of service. But the way of doing this is extremely difficult.'

Yet another slice of seemingly paradoxical wisdom! This quote suggests that the act of offering one's opinion and correcting faults is not just an exercise in ego, but a compassionate service. Yet, it warns us of the difficulty in doing so. This is particularly resonant in healthcare, where the stakes are high, and the ethical landscape is fraught with complexities.

The Importance of Individual and Institutional Honor

In the world of healthcare, honor isn't just a personal badge you wear; it's the ethical DNA that permeates your entire institution. The Hagakure teaches us that honor is like the ink in a well-crafted calligraphy piece; it flows from the individual to the collective, leaving an indelible mark on everyone and everything it touches. It's not just about you; it's about how your actions reverberate through the hallways of your hospital, the policies of your clinic, or the curriculum of your medical school.

Imagine honor as the family crest or the mon of your healthcare institution. This crest isn't just a decorative emblem; it's a living, breathing symbol that embodies the core values, ethics, and reputation of your organization. When you make an honorable decision—whether it's advocating for a patient, adhering to ethical guidelines, or standing up against malpractice—you're not just polishing your own armor; you're adding luster to that collective crest.

This sense of collective responsibility is what sets healthcare apart. Your actions, honorable or otherwise, don't exist in a vacuum. They influence patient outcomes, staff morale, and public perception. They shape institutional policies and can even set precedents that last for generations. It's a shared ethos, a communal code of conduct that turns individual actions into collective milestones or, if we're not careful, collective failures.

So, when we talk about honor in healthcare, we're talking about a multi-layered, far-reaching concept that goes beyond individual accolades or isolated acts of bravery. We're talking about a foundational principle that shapes the ethical landscape of entire institutions. It's a tall order, but then again, the path of honor was never meant to be easy. It's a journey that demands the wisdom of a seasoned samurai and the commitment of an entire clan. And in the high-stakes, emotionally charged arena of healthcare, could we really settle for anything less?

Accountability and Self-Reflection

Accountability and self-reflection are the twin pillars that hold up the temple of ethical healthcare. In the samurai tradition, the end of each day was a time for reflection, a moment to review one's actions and decisions, to weigh them against the code of Bushido. This wasn't just a casual glance in the rearview mirror; it was a deep, introspective dive into the soul, a reckoning with oneself. Can you imagine if healthcare providers adopted this samurai-like practice of nightly reflection? What transformations could occur?

Let's start with accountability. In healthcare, the stakes are sky-high. Lives hang in the balance, and the margin for error is razor-thin. When mistakes happen—and let's be real, they do—the easiest route is often to deflect blame, to point fingers, or worse, to sweep it under the rug. But is that the way of the samurai? Hardly. A samurai takes full responsibility for his actions, whether they result in victory or defeat. It's this unwavering accountability that sets the stage for ethical growth and learning. When you own your actions, you're not just acknowledging your fallibility; you're also honoring the trust that patients place in you. It's like polishing your armor after battle, ensuring you're better prepared for the next challenge.

Now, let's talk about self-reflection. In the fast-paced world of healthcare, who has the time to sit down and ponder, right? But what if I told you that this "waste of time" could be the most productive part of your day? Self-reflection is the forge where the samurai's sword of ethical clarity is tempered. It's the quiet space where you can dissect complex ethical dilemmas, untangle emotional knots, and gain insights that no medical textbook can offer. It's where you confront not just your actions but your motivations, asking yourself tough questions like, "Did I act in the patient's best interest?" or "Was I influenced by bias or external pressures?"

Self-reflection is essential for ethical healthcare providers, but let's get real - some days you barely have time to eat, let alone ponder deep philosophical questions! Still, try to intentionally build in mindful minutes of introspection where possible. Even taking 30 seconds between patients to close your eyes and take some deep breaths can help center your ethical compass.

Picture this: At the end of a grueling day, you sit down for a moment of reflection. You replay the day's events, not just the medical decisions but the ethical ones. Did you give each patient your full attention, or were you mentally ticking off your to-do list? When faced with an ethical dilemma, did you take the easy way out, or did you grapple with it, samurai-style, seeking a solution that honored both your integrity and the patient's dignity? This isn't just navel-gazing; it's an ethical audit, a personal inventory that can reveal both your strengths and your blind spots.

Just be sure not to accidentally record your innermost doubts and insecurities in a patient's progress note! "After further reflection, I question if I'm actually cut out for this whole medicine thing??" would be an awkward addition to the chart, resulting in some interesting reviews from the ethics board. Keep those reflective journal entries separate! Focus on self-care and celebrate your incremental progress, even if you still feel lightyears away from achieving samurai-level honor.

So, what's the takeaway? Accountability and self-reflection aren't just lofty ideals; they're practical tools, as essential to your ethical toolkit as a stethoscope is to your medical practice. They're the practices that transform you from a healthcare provider into an ethical warrior, a modern-day samurai armed with the moral courage and wisdom to navigate the complex battleground of healthcare ethics. And just like the samurai who reflects nightly on his deeds, these practices become a ritual, a sacred space where you meet yourself, warts and all, and emerge not just a better healthcare provider, but a better human being.

Public Trust and Healthcare

Ah, the matter of public trust—a cornerstone that holds up the edifice of healthcare. Imagine it as the samurai's oath to protect his community, an unwavering commitment that goes beyond the battlefield and seeps into the very fabric of society. When you don the white coat, stethoscope, or nurse's scrubs, you're not just assuming a professional role; you're stepping into a position of public trust. And just like a samurai's honor reflects on his clan, your conduct reflects on the entire healthcare community.

But what happens when that trust is shaken? A single scandal, a lone act of negligence, or even a well-intentioned but misguided decision can ripple through the public consciousness like a sword through silk. The Hagakure teaches us that a samurai's actions are never just his own; they reflect on his master, his family, and his clan. Similarly, when one healthcare provider falters, the tremors are felt throughout the institution and, by extension, the entire profession. It's a collective responsibility, a shared burden of honor that we all carry.

So, how do we uphold this public trust? It starts with individual acts of integrity—being transparent with patients, adhering to evidence-based practices, respecting confidentiality, and so on. But it also extends to systemic practices. Are institutions fostering a culture of ethical excellence? Are there checks and balances to catch and correct errors? Is there a pathway for ethical concerns to be raised without fear of retribution?

The Hagakure offers a lesson here: "To give a person one's opinion and correct his faults is an important thing. It is compassionate and comes first in matters of service." In the context of healthcare, this could mean creating an environment where ethical dialogue is encouraged, where mistakes are treated as opportunities for growth rather than reasons for punishment. It's about building an institutional culture that values the ethical over the expedient, the just over the merely legal.

And let's not forget the role of communication in maintaining public trust. In an age where information can spread faster than wildfire, healthcare providers and institutions must be proactive in sharing accurate information, correcting misconceptions, and being transparent about both successes and failures. It's not just about "saving face"; it's about preserving the integrity of the healthcare system in the eyes of those it serves.

So, the next time you find yourself at an ethical crossroads, remember: the path you choose won't just affect you or your immediate patient. It will send ripples across the pond of public trust. And in that moment, let the wisdom of the Hagakure guide you. For in the delicate balance of honor and duty, you'll find the essence of ethical healthcare.

Transparency

Ah, transparency—the glass pane of healthcare ethics. On the surface, it seems straightforward: just be open, honest, and clear. But anyone who's navigated the labyrinthine corridors of healthcare knows it's rarely that simple. The Hagakure tells us, "To give a person one's opinion and correct his faults is an important thing. It is compassionate and comes first in matters of service." But how does this ancient wisdom translate into the modern healthcare setting, where the stakes are high and the ethical terrain is complex?

Imagine you're a doctor, and you've just realized a mistake was made during a procedure. Your first instinct, guided by the principle of transparency, might be to disclose the error to the patient immediately. It's the honorable thing to do, right? But here's where the samurai's sword of transparency becomes double-edged. What if your full disclosure causes unnecessary distress to the patient, or worse, erodes their trust in healthcare altogether? Is your transparency still a virtue, or has it become a vice?

Or consider a different scenario. You're a healthcare administrator privy to confidential information about an upcoming merger that could result in staff layoffs. Do you disclose this to your team, potentially causing panic and lowering morale, or do you keep it under wraps until you have all the facts? Here, transparency is a tightrope walk over a chasm of ethical dilemmas, each step requiring careful balance and keen judgment.

The Hagakure offers a nuanced perspective: "Matters of great concern should be treated lightly. Matters of small concern should be treated seriously." In other words, the weight of the issue should guide the level of transparency. Critical matters that directly impact patient care demand a higher level of openness, while less critical issues may warrant a more measured approach. It's not about withholding information but about delivering it in a way that serves the greater good.

But let's not forget, transparency isn't just about what you reveal; it's also about how you reveal it. It's the art of communication, the skill of conveying complex medical jargon in terms that a layperson can understand. It's about creating a safe space where patients feel comfortable asking questions and voicing concerns. And it's about being honest when you don't have all the answers, acknowledging the limitations of medicine and the uncertainties that come with it.

So, is full disclosure always the most honorable route? Not necessarily. Like a masterful samurai, you must read the situation, understand the stakes, and act in a way that upholds both your honor and the well-being of those you serve. Transparency, in this sense, isn't a one-size-fits-all mandate; it's a flexible ethical principle that adapts to the contours of each unique healthcare encounter.

In the end, transparency is less about the act of revealing and more about the art of understanding—understanding when to speak, how to speak, and what impact your words will have. It's a dance of ethics and empathy, choreographed to the timeless wisdom of the Hagakure. And when performed with skill and honor, it's a dance that enriches not just the individual but the entire healthcare community.

Implications for Whistleblowing

Whistleblowing in healthcare is akin to a samurai unsheathing his sword in a crowded marketplace. It's a dramatic, consequential act, one that demands the utmost courage and conviction. The Hagakure tells us that honor often requires us to make difficult, even perilous choices. When you blow the whistle, you're embodying this ancient wisdom, standing as a sentinel of the principle of "doing no harm." You're choosing to protect patients, uphold ethical standards, and in some cases, save lives. It's the ultimate act of loyalty to the very essence of healthcare.

But let's not romanticize it too much. This sword of truth is double-edged. While you're cutting through malpractice or unethical behavior, you're also exposing yourself to potential backlash. You risk being labeled a dissident, a troublemaker, or even a traitor to your institution. Your reputation may suffer, professional relationships could fray, and yes, your job might hang in the balance. It's as if the very act of drawing your sword puts you at risk of falling on it.

This is where the Hagakure's teachings on honor become a crucial guide. True honor isn't about taking the easy path; it's about navigating the treacherous terrain of ethical dilemmas with your integrity intact. It's about being prepared to make sacrifices, to face the potential repercussions head-on, all in the name of what's right. It's a test, not just of your ethical convictions but of your inner resolve.

Remember the samurai wisdom that has endured for centuries. Know that the path of honor is fraught with challenges that will test your mettle, just as a samurai's sword is tested in the heat of battle. But also know that by walking this path, you're not just defending your own honor; you're upholding the honor of your profession and your institution. It's a heavy burden, but one that the truly honorable are prepared to bear.

Moral Courage

The unsung hero of ethical healthcare. Picture it as the lone samurai standing defiantly against an overwhelming force, his eyes steely, his grip firm on the hilt of his sword. He knows the odds are against him, but he stands his ground because his cause is just, his principles unyielding. This is the epitome of moral courage, a quality as vital to healthcare as surgical skill or medical knowledge.

But what does moral courage look like in the corridors of a hospital or the rooms of a clinic? It's the nurse who speaks up when she sees a colleague cutting corners in patient care, even if it risks workplace tension. It's the doctor who refuses to bend to administrative pressure to discharge a patient before it's medically advisable. It's the healthcare worker who, amid a pandemic, insists on proper safety protocols even when resources are stretched thin. These are the modern-day samurais, the guardians of healthcare ethics, standing their ground in the face of adversity.

The Hagakure tells us, "There is something to be learned from a rainstorm... When meeting with a sudden shower, you try not to get wet and run quickly along the road. But doing such things as passing under the eaves of houses, you still get wet. When you are resolved from the beginning, you will not be perplexed, though you will still get the same soaking." In other words, moral courage isn't about avoiding challenges or conflicts; it's about facing them head-on, with resolve and clarity.

But let's be real—moral courage is hard. It's emotionally taxing and can be professionally risky. You might be labeled as a troublemaker, or worse, find your job on the line. So, why do it? Because the cost of silence, of ethical inaction, is far greater. It's a stain on your honor, a tarnish on the ethical crest of your healthcare institution, and a breach in the dam of public trust. And once that dam breaks, it's not easy to rebuild.

So, how do you cultivate this brand of courage? It starts with self-awareness, with understanding your own ethical principles and boundaries. It's fortified by education and mentorship, by learning from the ethical samurais who've walked the path before you. And it's sustained by a supportive community, by fostering a healthcare environment where ethics are discussed, debated, and held in the highest regard.

The next time you find yourself at an ethical impasse, remember the lone samurai. Feel the weight of your metaphorical sword, take a deep breath, and make your stand. For in that moment of moral courage, you're not just preserving your own honor; you're upholding the integrity of healthcare itself.

Ethical Leadership and Reputation Management

As an ethical leader, remember that your actions reflect on the whole institution, so be on your best behavior! Leave the whiskey-fueled carousing to the wild college kids - you set the tone now. Save your inner rebel for more reputable acts of harmless non-conformity, like impromptu karaoke at office parties or adopting an unusual pet. But even then, keep social media posts tactful. Lead by example, and don't become a headline.

Leadership in healthcare is a role that goes far beyond the confines of administrative duties or resource management. It's akin to being a samurai general on the battlefield of ethics and morality. Just as a general's conduct sets the standard for his troops, your ethical comportment sets the tone for the entire institution you represent. You're not just a manager; you're a moral compass, a beacon that guides the ethical behavior of everyone from the janitorial staff to the board of directors.

Imagine, if you will, a samurai general standing tall on a hill, overlooking the battlefield. His posture, his gaze, even the way he holds his sword—everything about him communicates a message to his troops. It's a message of unwavering integrity, of a commitment to honor that goes beyond mere words. Now, translate that image to a healthcare setting. Your actions, your decisions, and yes, even your mistakes, serve as lessons in ethical conduct for your team. You're setting the stage for an ethical culture, one that can either elevate your institution or erode its foundations.

And let's not forget the strategic importance of ethical leadership. We live in an age where a single tweet can tarnish a reputation built over decades. Patient reviews, social media chatter, and public perception can significantly impact an institution's standing. Ethical missteps don't just risk legal repercussions; they can lead to a loss of public trust that's devastatingly hard to rebuild. In this context, ethical leadership isn't just a lofty ideal; it's a strategic imperative. It's about safeguarding not just the moral integrity of your institution, but its reputation and viability in a fiercely competitive landscape.

When you're faced with an ethical decision, remember that you're not just making a choice for yourself or even for a single patient. You're making a choice that will ripple through your entire institution, influencing perceptions, behaviors, and ultimately, the very ethos of your healthcare setting. It's a responsibility that demands the wisdom, courage, and integrity of a seasoned samurai.

Integrity and the Art of the Apology

An apology—a simple act, yet fraught with complexity, especially in the realm of healthcare. It's like the samurai's bow, a gesture that can convey respect, humility, and honor, but also one that can be misinterpreted, especially when cultural nuances come into play. So, what's the deal with apologies in healthcare? Are they a sign of weakness, an admission of guilt, or could they be something more, something that elevates the ethical landscape?

In Western cultures, particularly in the litigious environment of the United States, an apology can be a double-edged sword. On one side, it's a powerful tool for mending fences, for acknowledging a mistake and taking the first step toward making amends. It's the honorable thing to do, akin to a samurai openly admitting a tactical error. But on the flip side, that same apology can be seen as an admission of guilt, a legal liability that could come back to haunt you. It's a delicate dance, one that requires the finesse and timing of a samurai entering battle.

Now, let's take a detour to Eastern cultures, where the apology often carries a different weight. In Japan, for instance, apologizing is deeply ingrained in the culture, a social lubricant that smooths over conflicts and maintains harmony. It's less about admitting fault and more about acknowledging the social disruption caused by the event. In this context, an apology isn't just an individual act; it's a collective gesture that upholds the social fabric. It's like the samurai who bows not just to show respect but to acknowledge his place in the larger social order.

So, how does this all translate to healthcare? Imagine you're a healthcare provider who's made an error. Your Western training might make you hesitant to apologize, fearing legal repercussions. But what if an apology, carefully worded and sincerely delivered, could actually defuse tension and pave the way for constructive dialogue? What if it could restore not just the patient's trust in you, but also their faith in the healthcare system at large?

And let's not forget the therapeutic potential of an apology. For patients and families, an apology can be a balm for emotional wounds, a first step in the healing process. It acknowledges their suffering and validates their experience, sending a powerful message: "I see you, and I take responsibility." It's a moment of ethical grace, a point where compassion and justice intersect.

The Hagakure offers us a valuable lesson here: "To give a person one's opinion and correct his faults is an important thing. It is compassionate and comes first in matters of service." Could an apology be a form of compassionate service, a way to correct faults and restore honor?

Navigating the ethical terrain of apologies in healthcare is no simple task. It requires the wisdom of a seasoned samurai and the sensitivity of a diplomat. But when done right, an apology can be a transformative act, a manifestation of both honor and integrity. It's not just about saying "I'm sorry"; it's about understanding the weight those words carry and the ripples they send through the ethical landscape. So the next time you find yourself in a situation that calls for an apology, take a moment to consider not just the risks, but also the opportunities. Your ethical self will thank you.

The Concept of "Saving Face"

In Eastern cultures, the notion of "saving face" is complex. It's not just about you; it's about the collective, the community, the greater good. Picture it as the samurai's code of conduct, a set of unwritten rules that govern not just individual actions but the social fabric itself. Now, let's transport this concept into the healthcare setting, where the stakes are not just reputational but literally life and death.

Imagine you're a healthcare provider who's made an error—a medication mix-up, perhaps. The Western approach might prioritize full disclosure, immediate apology, and corrective action. But in a culture that values "saving face," the approach might be more nuanced. It could involve a careful balancing act between admitting fault and preserving the dignity of all involved—patients, families, and healthcare providers. It's like a samurai who must admit a mistake in battle; the admission is not just about him but reflects on his entire clan and even his lord.

This dance of "saving face" extends to all aspects of healthcare, from the way patient complaints are managed to how team conflicts are resolved. It's not just about avoiding blame or embarrassment. It's about maintaining an ethical equilibrium within the healthcare community. It's about ensuring that the honor and dignity of the institution are upheld, even when individual members falter.

The Hagakure offers that honor is not a solitary endeavor. It's a collective responsibility, a shared burden. Your actions, your choices, your mistakes—they don't just reflect on you. They ripple outwards, affecting the reputation and harmony of your entire healthcare community. In this context, "saving face" is not an act of vanity or self-preservation. It's an ethical duty, a commitment to uphold the collective honor of your institution.

As you find yourself in a situation where "saving face" seems at odds with transparency or accountability, remember the wisdom of the Hagakure. Consider that perhaps the most honorable course of action is one that maintains the delicate balance between individual dignity and collective harmony. It's a tightrope walk over the chasm of ethical dilemmas, one that requires the agility and wisdom of a samurai. Are you ready to walk that line?

As we delve into the complexities of honor and integrity in healthcare, let these principles guide you. It teaches us that honor is both a personal quest and a collective responsibility, a dual commitment to self and society. And in the challenging, ever-evolving landscape of healthcare ethics, what could be more important than that?

Ethical *Case Study* 5: Reporting a Colleague's Mistake: The Ethical Tightrope of Honor and Integrity

Introduction

In the bustling, high-stakes environment of a metropolitan hospital's Intensive Care Unit (ICU), Sally, a seasoned nurse with over a decade of experience, finds herself in a moral quagmire. During a particularly hectic shift, she witnesses her colleague, Mark, administer an incorrect dosage of a critical medication to a patient. The patient, already in a fragile state, could suffer severe consequences from this error.

Sally is now standing at an ethical crossroads. On one hand, she has an unwavering duty to ensure the safety and well-being of her patients—an oath she took when she entered the nursing profession. This path calls her to report the mistake immediately, thereby upholding the principle of honor that is so deeply ingrained in healthcare. On the other hand, Mark is not just a name on a staff roster; he's a human being, a friend, and a generally competent nurse who has been going through a rough patch personally. Reporting him could lead to disciplinary action, tarnish his professional reputation, and even jeopardize his career. This is where integrity comes into play.

The dilemma is further complicated by the close-knit nature of healthcare teams. Reporting Mark could strain team dynamics, affecting not just Sally and Mark but also their colleagues, who might start to question the trust they place in one another. The ripples of this single decision could extend far beyond the immediate situation, affecting team morale, patient care, and even the reputation of the institution they both serve.

In essence, Sally's decision is not just about choosing between two options; it's about navigating a complex web of ethical and interpersonal relationships. It's about balancing the scales of honor and integrity in a world where every choice comes with its own set of consequences. And it's about doing all this while bearing in mind that at the center of this ethical storm is a patient whose life hangs in the balance.

Background

Sally and Mark have been colleagues for over five years, working side by side in the ICU of St. Michael's Hospital, a renowned healthcare institution in the heart of the city. They've shared victories in saving lives and faced defeats in losing them. Over the years, they've built a rapport that goes beyond professional courtesy; they've become friends. Mark has been known as a diligent and competent nurse, but lately, he's been going through a difficult divorce, and the stress has started to show in his work.

The patient involved is Emily, a 45-year-old mother of two who was admitted for severe pneumonia complicated by other underlying health conditions. Her case is critical, and the medication in question is vital to stabilizing her condition. A mistake in dosage could lead to a range of adverse effects, from prolonged hospital stay to organ failure or even death.

The ICU is a high-stress environment, especially during the evening shifts when staffing is leaner, and both Sally and Mark are part of a team that is already stretched thin. The hospital administration has been pushing for higher efficiency metrics, adding another layer of stress to an already tense atmosphere. Mistakes can happen, but the stakes are incredibly high, given the critical nature of the patients they care for.

The hospital has a reporting system in place for medical errors, designed to be confidential and non-punitive. The aim is to encourage healthcare providers to report mistakes so that systemic issues can be identified and addressed. However, the reality is often more complicated. While the system is meant to be impartial, there's an unspoken understanding among staff that reporting a colleague could have serious repercussions for the individual reported, especially if the error is as significant as a medication mistake in the ICU.

Adding another layer of complexity is the hospital's recent push for a "culture of transparency and accountability," spurred by a few high-profile cases of medical malpractice that made headlines. The administration has been emphasizing the importance of ethical conduct and has even invited speakers to discuss the concept of honor in medical practice. This initiative has been met with mixed reactions from the staff, some of whom view it as mere lip service, while others see it as a step in the right direction.

In this intricate tapestry of professional, ethical, and personal dynamics, Sally must make a decision that aligns with both her moral compass and the ethical guidelines of her profession. It's a decision that will undoubtedly leave its mark, not just on her and Mark, but on their team, their patient, and perhaps even their institution.

Ethical Issues

At the heart of this dilemma lies a clash between two core ethical principles: the duty to ensure patient safety (honor) and the potential impact on a colleague's career and well-being (integrity). Sally is torn between her obligation to report Mark's error, which could prevent future mistakes and protect patients, and her concern for the repercussions that Mark might face professionally and personally.

The ethical issue is further complicated by the friendship between Sally and Mark. Does her personal relationship with him cloud her judgment or influence her ethical responsibility? Is she willing to risk a friendship for the sake of upholding professional standards?

Another layer of ethical complexity is added by the hospital's recent emphasis on a "culture of transparency and accountability." While the institution outwardly encourages reporting errors for systemic improvement, there's an unspoken tension among staff about the real-world implications of doing so. Reporting Mark could be seen as aligning with the hospital's new cultural push, but at what cost?

Moreover, there's the issue of timing. Mark's error is not just a one-off mistake; it's happening during a period when he's visibly stressed due to personal issues. Does the context of his life situation offer any ethical leeway, or does the critical nature of the ICU environment make the error inexcusable regardless of personal circumstances?

Finally, there's the patient, Emily, to consider. She's not just a case number but a mother of two whose life could be significantly impacted by a medication error. Does Sally's duty to protect her patient outweigh all other considerations?

In summary, Sally faces a multifaceted ethical issue that involves conflicting duties to her patient, her colleague, her institution, and even herself. It's a complex web of moral, professional, and personal considerations that demands a well-thought-out decision.

Stakeholders

Nurse Sally: Witness to the mistake, holds the ethical dilemma. Torn between her duty to ensure patient safety and her concern for her colleague's career.

Nurse Mark: Made the error, his career is at stake. Likely unaware of the mistake, stressed due to personal issues.

The Patient Emily: Health could be compromised due to the error. Unaware of the error, trusts healthcare providers for her well-being.

The Healthcare Institution: Reputation and legal standing could be affected.

Options

In this complex ethical landscape, Sarah has several courses of action, each with its own set of pros and cons that will impact the stakeholders differently.

Report the Error Immediately to Supervisors:

> **Pros:** Upholds the principle of patient safety. Aligns with hospital policy and ethical duty.

> **Cons:** Could severely damage Mark's career and reputation. May strain professional relationships within the team.

Confront Mark Privately First:

Pros: Gives Mark a chance to correct the error and learn from it. Maintains the integrity of the professional relationship.

Cons: Risks patient safety if Mark doesn't take corrective action. Puts Sarah in a precarious ethical position if Mark denies or ignores it.

Do Nothing and Monitor the Situation:

Pros: Avoids immediate conflict and potential harm to Mark's career. Buys time to consider the best course of action.

Cons: Compromises patient safety. Could be considered neglectful or unethical behavior on Sally's part.

Anonymously Report the Error:

Pros: Ensures patient safety without directly implicating Mark. Aligns with hospital policy.

Cons: May create an atmosphere of distrust within the team. Doesn't give Mark the opportunity for self-correction.

Each option comes with its own ethical weight and potential consequences for the stakeholders involved. Sarah's decision will not only reflect her own values but will also set a precedent for how similar ethical dilemmas are handled in the future within her healthcare team.

Ethical Analysis

In this intricate ethical scenario, Sally's options can be evaluated through various ethical theories and principles, including utilitarianism, deontology, virtue ethics, and care ethics. Additionally, the Hagakure's wisdom of making decisions "within the space of seven breaths" serves as a guiding principle.

Report the Error Immediately to Supervisors:

Utilitarianism: This option maximizes overall well-being by prioritizing patient safety, but at the cost of Mark's career.

Deontology: Aligns perfectly with the duty to uphold patient safety and adhere to hospital policy.

Virtue Ethics: Demonstrates courage and honesty but may lack compassion towards Mark.

Hagakure: This decisive action aligns with the principle of acting swiftly and with determination.

Confront Mark Privately First:

Utilitarianism: Could lead to the best overall outcome if Mark corrects his mistake.

Deontology: May conflict with the immediate duty to report errors that endanger patients.

Virtue Ethics: Shows compassion and gives Mark an opportunity for moral growth.

Hagakure: This approach is compassionate but difficult, aligning with the chapter's quote.

Do Nothing and Monitor the Situation:

Utilitarianism: Risks the worst overall outcome by endangering patient safety.

Deontology: Clearly violates the duty to the patient and to ethical practice.

Virtue Ethics: Demonstrates neither courage nor wisdom.

Hagakure: This indecisiveness is the antithesis of acting within "seven breaths."

Anonymously Report the Error:

Utilitarianism: Ensures patient safety but may create an atmosphere of distrust.

Deontology: Partially fulfills the duty to report but skirts around direct responsibility.

Virtue Ethics: May be seen as lacking in courage and honesty.

Hagakure: This action is swift but may lack the spirit of "breaking through to the other side" by not confronting the issue directly.

Each option presents its own ethical challenges and alignments with various theories. The Hagakure's principle of swift, determined action serves as a reminder that ethical dilemmas often require us to act quickly, yet thoughtfully, in the service of both self and others.

Recommend Course of Action

After a thorough ethical analysis, the recommended course of action is to confront Mark privately first, giving him the opportunity to correct his mistake and report it himself. This recommendation is based on a balanced consideration of ethical theories and the wisdom of the Hagakure.

Justification:

1. **Utilitarian Perspective**: This option has the potential for the best overall outcome. It allows for the mistake to be corrected, thereby ensuring patient safety, while also giving Mark the chance for ethical and professional growth.

2. **Deontological Perspective**: While immediate reporting aligns more closely with the duty to uphold patient safety, confronting Mark first respects the duty to treat colleagues with fairness and to foster an environment where mistakes are learning opportunities.

3. **Virtue Ethics**: This approach embodies several virtues, including compassion, wisdom, and courage. It gives Mark the opportunity for moral growth, which is a virtuous act in itself.

4. **Hagakure Wisdom**: The chapter's quote from the Hagakure emphasizes the difficulty but importance of compassionately correcting someone's faults. Confronting Mark aligns with this wisdom by taking the more difficult but compassionate route.

By choosing to confront Mark privately first, Sally would be acting in a manner that aligns with multiple ethical theories, while also embodying the wisdom of the Hagakure. It's a course of action that requires courage and compassion but is rooted in the spirit of ethical integrity and honor. It's about making a difficult decision swiftly but thoughtfully, embodying the Hagakure's principle of deciding "within the space of seven breaths."

Conclusion

This case study, "Reporting a Colleague's Mistake," delves into the intricate ethical landscape healthcare professionals often navigate. It presents a situation where the principles of honor and integrity are in tension, forcing Sarah to make a difficult decision that could have far-reaching implications. The ethical dilemma centers around whether to report a colleague's potentially harmful error immediately or confront the colleague first, thereby giving him an opportunity to correct his mistake.

The ethical issues at hand are multi-faceted, involving patient safety, professional integrity, and the moral development of healthcare providers. The key stakeholders include the patient, whose safety is paramount; Sarah, who is the witness to the error; and Mark, the colleague who made the mistake. Each of these stakeholders has something significant to gain or lose based on Sarah's decision.

Several options were considered, each with its own set of pros and cons. These options were then analyzed through the lens of various ethical theories, including utilitarianism, deontology, virtue ethics, and care ethics. The wisdom of the Hagakure was also invoked, emphasizing the importance and difficulty of correcting someone's faults compassionately.

The recommended course of action—confronting Mark privately first—was chosen for its balanced approach to the ethical dilemma. It respects the principles of patient safety and professional integrity while also allowing room for moral growth and compassionate interaction among colleagues. This recommendation is not just about making the "right" choice but about making a choice that embodies the virtues of honor and integrity, virtues that are deeply rooted in the teachings of the Hagakure.

In closing, this case study serves as a vivid illustration of the complexities involved in ethical decision-making in healthcare. It's a testament to the fact that ethical practice is not a checkbox exercise but a nuanced, ongoing journey. It's about making difficult decisions swiftly but thoughtfully, embodying the Hagakure's principle of deciding "within the space of seven breaths." And it's a reminder that the path of ethical practice is one that requires both honor and integrity, qualities that are not just professional requirements but life-long virtues.

Chapter 6: Embracing Challenges

'There is something to be learned from a rainstorm. When meeting with a sudden shower, you try not to get wet and run quickly along the road. By doing such things as passing under the eaves of houses, you still get wet. When you are resolved from the beginning, you will not be perplexed, though you still get the same soaking.'

The rainstorm is a metaphor as timeless as it is poignant. Imagine you're a healthcare provider, and the rainstorm is an ethical dilemma that suddenly bursts into your day. You could try to dodge the raindrops, seeking refuge under the eaves of protocol or precedent. But let's be honest: you're still going to get wet. Ethical dilemmas are like that; they seep into the fabric of healthcare, leaving no one untouched. So, why not embrace the rain?

The Hagakure tells us, "When you are resolved from the beginning, you will not be perplexed, though you still get the same soaking." It's a call to arms—or perhaps, a call to heart. It urges us to face ethical challenges with resolve, to wade into the murky waters of moral complexity with our ethical swords unsheathed. It's not about avoiding the rain but learning how to dance in it.

The Ethical Clinician's Mindset

Ah, the Ethical Clinician's Mindset—what a compelling concept! Picture yourself as a samurai, not in feudal Japan, but in the bustling hallways of a modern hospital. Your armor isn't made of steel and leather; it's forged from years of rigorous education, countless hours of clinical training, and the wisdom gleaned from mentors and experiences. It's an armor imbued with the ethical theories you've studied and the moral dilemmas you've wrestled with. It's your first line of defense against the ethical onslaughts that healthcare inevitably throws your way.

Now, let's talk about your sword. It's not just a piece of sharpened metal; it's an extension of your very being. In the samurai's world, the sword is the soul. In your world, the sword represents your ethical principles—autonomy, beneficence, non-maleficence, and justice. These principles are your weapons, finely honed through years of ethical quandaries and moral debates. They're what you wield when you're plunged into the thick of ethical combat, be it a complex end-of-life decision, a tricky resource allocation issue, or a gnarly conflict of interest.

But what good is a sword if you don't know how to use it? That's where your moral compass comes in. This isn't a gadget you can buy; it's an internal navigation system that's been calibrated through years of ethical exploration. It's what guides your sword arm when you're in the heat of battle, helping you slice through the complexities and contradictions that muddy the ethical waters. Your moral compass is your inner samurai, the voice that whispers the Hagakure's wisdom in your ear: "Be resolved, and you will not be perplexed."

So, when an ethical storm clouds your horizon, you don't look for the nearest shelter; you draw your sword. You confront the challenge head-on, not with fear but with resolve. You wade into the murky waters of moral ambiguity, guided by a compass that points steadfastly toward ethical north. You make the hard decisions, the gut-wrenching choices that keep lesser warriors awake at night. And you do it all with the poise and confidence of a samurai who knows that his armor is strong, his sword is sharp, and his compass is true.

That, my friends, is the Ethical Clinician's Mindset. It's not a state of being but a **way** of being; a conscious choice to face ethical challenges with the courage of a samurai and the wisdom of a sage. So, the next time you find yourself at an ethical crossroads, remember: you're a clinical warrior, armed and ready. All you must do is draw your sword.

The Art of Ethical Decision-Making

Ah, the art of ethical decision-making! Imagine it as the samurai's kata, a choreographed sequence of movements that, to the untrained eye, may appear straightforward, even simplistic. But you, the seasoned practitioner, know better. Each movement in the kata is a distillation of years of training, each stance a testament to countless hours of practice. The kata isn't just a series of movements; it's a physical expression of the samurai's philosophy, a dance of ethics and skill.

Similarly, ethical decision-making in healthcare isn't a matter of following a checklist or adhering to a rigid set of rules. It's a nuanced dance that requires a deep understanding of ethical principles, a keen sense of empathy, and a razor-sharp ability to reason morally. It's a blend of logic and emotion, a delicate balancing act that demands both intellectual rigor and emotional intelligence. You're not just applying rules; you're interpreting them, adapting them to the unique contours of each ethical landscape you encounter.

So, how do you master this intricate dance? The same way the samurai masters his kata: through relentless practice and continuous learning. Each ethical dilemma you face is a new movement to add to your kata, a unique challenge that helps you refine your technique and deepen your understanding of ethical principles. It's a chance to test your moral mettle, to pit your ethical reasoning against the complexities and contradictions of the real world.

But here's the kicker: the learning never stops. Just as the samurai continually refines his kata, adding new movements and discarding those that no longer serve him, you too must remain open to growth, willing to adapt your ethical framework to the ever-changing landscape of healthcare. It's an ongoing process, a never-ending journey toward ethical mastery.

Embrace ethical challenges as a learning opportunity, a chance to practice your ethical kata. Approach it with the humility of a student and the wisdom of a master, knowing that each decision you make, each action you take, is a brushstroke in the ever-evolving art of ethical healthcare. And remember, the path to mastery is paved with challenges. The question is, are you ready to embrace them?

The Role of Resilience

Resilience is truly the unsung hero of ethical healthcare. Picture it as the samurai's indomitable spirit, the unyielding resolve that allows him to face any adversary, no matter how formidable. In healthcare, ethical dilemmas are your adversaries, as inevitable and unpredictable as a sudden rainstorm. You can't avoid them, and sometimes, you can't even prepare for them. They hit you when you least expect it, soaking you to the bone, challenging your ethical integrity, and testing your moral resolve.

But here's where resilience comes into play. It's not just a raincoat to shield you from the storm; it's the inner fortitude that allows you to stand tall, drenched yet undaunted. Resilience is what enables you to navigate through the tempest of ethical dilemmas without losing your way, to get soaked yet still stand firm in your ethical convictions. It's the quality that allows you to look yourself in the mirror after the storm has passed and say, "I did the best I could, given the circumstances."

But let's dig deeper. Resilience isn't just about weathering the storm; it's about learning from it, growing stronger through each drop that falls. Every ethical dilemma you face is a raindrop, a unique challenge that has the potential to erode your ethical foundation. But with resilience, these raindrops become lessons, opportunities to reinforce and strengthen that foundation. They become the building blocks of ethical wisdom, the raw material that you use to construct a more robust, more resilient ethical framework.

So, how do you cultivate this kind of resilience? The same way the samurai cultivates his spirit: through constant practice, relentless self-examination, and an unwavering commitment to ethical growth. It's a lifelong endeavor, a never-ending quest for ethical enlightenment. And just like the samurai, you'll face setbacks along the way, moments when the storm seems too fierce, the ethical dilemmas too overwhelming. But that's precisely when resilience matters most. It's the inner strength that allows you to stand firm, to face the storm head-on and emerge on the other side, not just intact but stronger, wiser, and more ethically resilient than before.

So, the next time you find yourself in the midst of an ethical downpour, don't run for cover. Stand tall, let the raindrops fall, and know that each one is an opportunity for growth, a challenge to be embraced, a lesson to be learned. That's the power of resilience, the indomitable spirit that turns ethical dilemmas into stepping stones on the path to ethical mastery. Are you ready to embrace the rain yet?

The Ethical Team: Collective Wisdom

Ah, the collective wisdom of the team—a concept as ancient as the samurai's code of Bushido, yet as relevant as today's multidisciplinary healthcare settings. Imagine, if you will, a samurai heading into battle. He's not charging in alone, sword swinging wildly. No, he's part of a unit, a collective force where each warrior brings a unique skill set to the table. There's the archer with his keen eye, the cavalryman with his speed, and the strategist with his tactical acumen. Together, they form a balanced, well-rounded team, each member's strengths compensating for the others' weaknesses.

Now, let's bring this back to the healthcare arena. When you're faced with an ethical dilemma, you're not just a lone samurai grappling with a moral quandary. You're part of a healthcare team, a collective force composed of doctors, nurses, ethicists, administrators, and sometimes even the patients and their families. Each member brings a unique perspective to the table, a distinct lens through which to view the ethical dilemma at hand.

Why is this collective approach so crucial? Because ethical dilemmas are complex beasts, multifaceted puzzles that rarely have a single "right" answer. They're like the mythical hydras of ancient lore, sprouting new heads each time you think you've solved them. Tackling them alone is not just daunting; it's downright dangerous. You risk falling into ethical blind spots, those murky areas where your own biases and limitations obscure the full scope of the dilemma.

But when you approach ethical decision-making as a team, you create a safeguard against these blind spots. The doctor's medical expertise complements the nurse's patient-centric perspective. The ethicist's theoretical knowledge balances the administrator's practical concerns. And the patient's lived experience adds a layer of authenticity and urgency that no healthcare provider can replicate. It's a symphony of perspectives, each contributing a unique note to the ethical melody.

This collective wisdom doesn't just make the decision-making process more robust; it makes it more ethical. It ensures that the decisions you make are not just medically sound but morally justifiable, not just practical but compassionate. It's like having a moral GPS that's constantly recalibrating, drawing on multiple data points to find the most ethical path forward.

So, the next time you find yourself entangled in an ethical dilemma, don't go it alone. Assemble your team, tap into that collective wisdom, and tackle the challenge head-on. It's not just the smart thing to do; it's the ethical thing to do. After all, even the most skilled samurai knows the value of fighting alongside trusted allies. Are you ready to embrace the collective wisdom of your healthcare team?

Ethics of Sacrifice

Ah, the Ethics of Sacrifice—a concept as weighty as the samurai's daisho, the paired long and short swords that symbolize his honor and duty. When you're in the healthcare arena, you're often faced with decisions that demand sacrifices, either personal or institutional. These are the moments that test your mettle, where you must decide what you're willing to give up for the sake of a higher ethical principle.

Imagine you're a healthcare administrator, and you're faced with a budget cut. You have a decision, maintaining a high standard of patient care or cutting corners to save money. The easy way out? Slash the budget, compromise on quality, and keep the higher-ups happy. But as a samurai of healthcare ethics, you know that's not an option. You're willing to risk your job, your reputation, even your career trajectory, to uphold the principles of quality care and patient safety. It's akin to a samurai choosing to fall on his sword rather than betray his lord or his code of honor.

Or consider a nurse who witnesses a colleague making a potentially harmful mistake. Reporting it could mean strained relationships, a hostile work environment, or even professional repercussions. But the nurse understands that the greater good—patient safety—must come first. It's a personal sacrifice, a risk to one's own well-being for the sake of upholding an ethical principle.

The Hagakure tells us, "The Way of the Samurai is found in death." It's a dramatic statement, but what it really means is that a samurai finds his true path when he's willing to face the ultimate sacrifice. In healthcare, the stakes may not always be life and death, but the sacrifices can be significant. Whether it's risking your job, your reputation, or even your personal relationships, these sacrifices are the price of maintaining your ethical integrity.

So how do you make these tough calls? First, you consult your ethical "sword," (hopefully honed sharp by years of training and experience!). You weigh the pros and cons, consider the broader implications, and listen to the wisdom of trusted colleagues. Then, with a deep breath, you make your decision, knowing full well the potential sacrifices that lie ahead.

But here's the thing: when you make a sacrifice for the right reasons, you're not just losing something. You're gaining something invaluable—the respect of your peers, the trust of your patients, and the inner peace that comes from knowing you've done the right thing. It's a form of ethical alchemy, turning the lead of sacrifice into the gold of integrity.

When you're faced with an ethical dilemma that demands a sacrifice, remember the samurai. Take up your ethical sword, weigh your options carefully, and be prepared to make the tough call. Because sometimes, falling on your sword is the most honorable thing you can do.

The Challenge of Timing

The concept of 'Right Timing,' or what the Japanese might call "*ima*," is as crucial in healthcare ethics as it is in the art of the samurai. It's the idea that there's an optimal moment for every action, a sweet spot where ethics, opportunity, and consequences align. Think of it as the samurai's perfect sword stroke, executed with precision and impeccable timing, cutting through ambiguity to reveal the ethical core of a situation.

In healthcare, 'Right Timing' is often the difference between a good decision and a disastrous one. Let's say you're a physician faced with an ethical dilemma—perhaps you've discovered that a new medication has severe side effects that haven't yet been disclosed to the public. Do you blow the whistle immediately, potentially causing panic and backlash? Or do you wait for more data, risking further harm to patients in the meantime? The 'Right Timing' here isn't just about what you do; it's about when you do it.

Or consider end-of-life decisions, a realm where timing is often fraught with ethical complexity. When is the right time to discuss palliative care options or to discontinue life-sustaining treatments? Too early, and you risk taking away hope; too late, and you may prolong suffering unnecessarily. The 'Right Timing' in such cases requires a blend of medical expertise, ethical reasoning, and a deep understanding of the patient's wishes and condition.

The Hagakure advises, "Throughout your life, advance daily, becoming more skillful than yesterday, more skillful than today. This is never-ending." In the same vein, mastering the concept of 'Right Timing' in healthcare ethics is a lifelong pursuit. It's not something you get right once and then forget about; it's a skill that requires constant honing, constant questioning, and a willingness to learn from both successes and failures.

How do you cultivate this sense of 'Right Timing'? First, you need to be fully present, attuned not just to the facts of the situation but also to the subtler cues—emotional, social, even spiritual—that might influence the outcome. You need to consult your ethical principles, yes, but also your intuition, your gut sense of what feels 'right' in this particular moment. And you need to be prepared to act, decisively and courageously, when that moment arrives.

In the world of the samurai, timing could mean the difference between life and death. In healthcare, the stakes are often just as high. Whether it's deciding when to speak up about an ethical concern, when to escalate care, or when to let go, 'Right Timing' is an essential skill for any healthcare provider. It's the moment when preparation meets opportunity, allowing you to cut through ethical dilemmas with the precision of a samurai's blade. So the next time you're faced with a tough ethical decision, don't just ask what the right thing to do is—ask when is the right time to do it.

The Challenge of Moral Resilience

Moral resilience—now there's a term that should be as familiar to healthcare providers as the hilt of a sword is to a samurai. It's not just about bouncing back from ethical dilemmas; it's about emerging from them stronger, wiser, and more ethically agile. Imagine a samurai who faces countless battles, each one teaching him something new about strategy, courage, and honor. Over time, he doesn't just survive these battles; he thrives, becoming a more skilled and confident warrior. That's moral resilience in action.

What's the secret to build this kind of moral stamina? Well, first, let's acknowledge that healthcare is a battlefield of its own, fraught with ethical landmines that can test even the most seasoned professionals. You're constantly navigating issues like patient autonomy, resource allocation, and end-of-life decisions, often under immense pressure. It's like being a samurai who's outnumbered, outgunned, and still expected to uphold the Bushido code.

The first step in building moral resilience is self-awareness. You need to know your own ethical boundaries, your own triggers, and your own blind spots. This is akin to a samurai knowing his weapon—its weight, its balance, its edge. When you're aware of your own ethical landscape, you can navigate challenges more effectively, avoiding the pitfalls that can lead to moral distress or burnout.

Next comes ethical training and education. Just as a samurai practices his swordsmanship daily, healthcare providers need ongoing training in ethics. This isn't a one-and-done deal; it's a lifelong commitment. Whether it's through formal ethics courses, case study discussions, or ethical rounds, continuous learning helps sharpen your ethical acumen, preparing you for the challenges ahead.

But what about when you're in the thick of it, facing an ethical dilemma that threatens to overwhelm you? This is where moral resilience really comes into play. It's the ability to stay grounded, to consult your ethical principles even when emotions are running high, and to make a decision that you can stand by, even if it's unpopular or risky. It's the samurai's unwavering focus in the heat of battle, the ability to tune out distractions and zero in on the ethical core of the situation.

And let's not forget the role of community. No samurai, no matter how skilled, goes to battle alone. Similarly, moral resilience is often a collective effort, bolstered by the support and wisdom of colleagues, mentors, and even patients. When you're unsure of the right course of action, seek out other perspectives. A well-rounded view can provide invaluable insights, helping you make a more informed—and more ethical—decision.

Finally, moral resilience involves reflection and self-care. After the battle is won—or lost—it's crucial to reflect on what went right, what went wrong, and what could be done differently next time. This is your moment for ethical self-care, a chance to recharge your moral batteries and prepare for the next challenge. Just as a samurai would clean and sharpen his sword after a battle, so too must healthcare providers maintain their ethical toolkit, ensuring it's ready for whatever comes next.

When facing your next ethical storm, remember the concept of moral resilience. It's your ethical armor, forged through self-awareness, honed through education, and tested through experience. With it, you'll not only survive the challenges of healthcare ethics; you'll thrive, emerging as a stronger, wiser, and more morally resilient version of yourself.

Don't run from the rain; embrace it. Equip yourself with the armor of knowledge and the sword of ethical principles and face the storm with the resolve of a true ethical warrior. Because sometimes, getting wet is the only way to appreciate the rain.

Ethical Case Study 6: Rationing Healthcare: The Ethics of Prioritizing Lives in a Pandemic

Introduction

The COVID-19 pandemic has been an unprecedented global crisis, affecting every facet of human life. One of the most pressing challenges has been its impact on healthcare systems. Hospitals have been stretched thin, facing a surge of patients that has often exceeded their capacity to provide care. This has led to a scarcity of essential medical resources—ventilators, ICU beds, medications, and even medical staff. In such a dire situation, healthcare providers are forced into the uncomfortable position of playing God, having to decide who gets access to life-saving treatment and who does not.

This case study delves into this ethical quagmire, focusing on a large urban hospital at the epicenter of a COVID-19 outbreak. The ICU is overflowing, medical staff are exhausted, and there's just one ventilator left. Several patients could benefit from it, but who should get it? Is it the young mother of three who has a higher likelihood of survival, or the elderly gentleman who came in first? Or perhaps it should go to someone who has been fully vaccinated?

The stakes are incredibly high. Lives hang in the balance, and the decisions made in these crucial moments will have ripple effects, not just for the patients and their families, but for society at large. It's a scenario that encapsulates the essence of ethical dilemmas in healthcare—decisions that are not just about medical facts, but about values, ethics, and the kind of society we want to be.

In this high-pressure, emotionally charged environment, the wisdom of the Hagakure offers a guiding light. It teaches us to make decisions "within the space of seven breaths," a principle that encourages swift yet thoughtful action. This case study aims to explore how such ancient wisdom can inform modern medical ethics, helping healthcare providers navigate the stormy seas of ethical dilemmas with the moral compass of a seasoned samurai.

Background

The setting is St. Ethica's Hospital, a large urban healthcare facility that has been serving a diverse community for decades. Located in the heart of a city hit hard by the COVID-19 pandemic, the hospital has been on the front lines since the outbreak began. The staff are a mix of seasoned professionals and young recruits, all united by a common mission but divided by the ethical challenges they face daily. The hospital's ICU is at full capacity, and the emergency room is a revolving door of critical cases.

The hospital has a triage protocol, but it was designed for more "normal" emergencies, not for a prolonged crisis of this magnitude. The ethical guidelines that usually serve as the hospital's moral compass are now being stretched to their limits. The hospital's ethics committee has been meeting more frequently to provide guidance, but the rapidly evolving situation often outpaces their ability to make recommendations.

Enter Dr. White, an experienced critical care physician, and Nurse Ahmed, a compassionate healthcare provider. They are the ones who must make the immediate, life-or-death decisions. They have been working back-to-back shifts, fueled by adrenaline, caffeine, and the acute awareness of the weight of their responsibilities.

The dilemma arises when two patients are admitted almost simultaneously. One is Rachel, a 35-year-old mother of three young children, with no underlying health conditions. She's been fully vaccinated but has contracted a severe case of COVID-19. The other is Mr. Thompson, a 70-year-old man with a history of respiratory issues. He was one of the first to be admitted during this surge and has been waiting longer for a ventilator. Both are in critical condition and would significantly benefit from the last available ventilator.

Adding another layer of complexity is a third patient, Matt, a 40-year-old unvaccinated individual who is also in critical condition. He had been vocal about his vaccine hesitancy and now finds himself in need of the same ventilator.

The clock is ticking, resources are dwindling, and the healthcare providers must make a decision that they will undoubtedly carry with them for the rest of their lives. This is not just a medical decision; it's an ethical one, fraught with moral, social, and even political implications. It's a decision that will be scrutinized, debated, and will set a precedent for future ethical dilemmas. And it's a decision that must be made now.

In the midst of this chaos, the Hagakure's wisdom echoes in the minds of our healthcare providers: "When you are resolved from the beginning, you will not be perplexed, though you still get the same soaking." It's a call to embrace the challenge, to make a decision with both urgency and ethical clarity—a samurai's resolve in the face of life's rainstorms.

Ethical Issues

At the crux of this case are four pivotal ethical quandaries:

Patient Priority vs. Personal Choice: The healthcare team is caught between the duty to allocate resources where they are most likely to save a life (honor) and respecting Mark's personal choice to remain unvaccinated (autonomy). Is it ethical to deprioritize Mark based on a personal choice he made, knowing that doing so could cost him his life?

Fairness vs. Utility: The team must also grapple with the principle of fairness—should each patient have an equal shot at the ventilator? This is complicated by the principle of utility, which suggests giving the ventilator to the patient most likely to benefit from it, such as Emily, who is younger and has dependent children. Is it fair to weigh these factors, or does it introduce a form of ethical bias?

Institutional Policy vs. Individual Judgment: The hospital has guidelines for resource allocation, but these are not always clear-cut and may not cover every unique situation. Does the healthcare team follow the institutional policy to the letter, or do they exercise individual clinical judgment? And who bears the responsibility for this decision?

Immediate Need vs. Long-term Consequences: The healthcare team is working under extreme pressure to make a quick decision, aligning with the Hagakure's principle of acting "within the space of seven breaths." However, the long-term ethical implications of this decision could reverberate through the lives of the patients, their families, and the healthcare providers themselves. How does one balance the urgency of the now with the ethical ramifications of the future?

Each of these ethical issues presents a complex interplay of moral, professional, and even existential considerations. The healthcare team is not just making a medical decision; they're making a profoundly ethical one that will leave an indelible mark on the lives involved. It's a high-stakes, high-pressure scenario that demands not just clinical expertise but also ethical wisdom.

Stakeholders

The Healthcare Team: Comprising doctors, nurses, and other medical professionals, this group is responsible for making the immediate decision about ventilator allocation.

They are ethically bound to do what's best for their patients but also must consider institutional policies and societal norms.

Matt: An unvaccinated patient in critical condition. His personal choice to remain unvaccinated puts him at odds with many who believe that healthcare resources should be allocated to those who have taken all available precautions. He's not just a patient; he's also a symbol of a divisive societal issue.

Rachel: A vaccinated mother of two who is also in critical condition. She represents the patient who has followed public health guidelines and yet finds herself in a life-threatening situation. Her young children and family add another layer of ethical complexity to the decision-making process.

The Hospital Administration: They are responsible for the policies that guide such decisions. While they may not be directly involved in this specific case, the outcome could have implications for future policy revisions and public relations.

Families of the Patients: They are emotionally invested stakeholders who may or may not have a say in the decision-making process. Their perspectives could range from understanding the complexities of the situation to feeling that their loved one was unfairly treated.

The Public: In the age of social media, any decision could become public knowledge, affecting societal trust in healthcare institutions. The public's view on how such ethical dilemmas should be handled can influence future policy and legislation.

Ethical Committees and Regulatory Bodies: These organizations may review the case after the fact and could impose sanctions or provide guidelines that influence future decisions.

The Legal System: Depending on the outcome, there could be legal repercussions that affect not only the healthcare providers but also the institution they represent.

Options

Prioritize Rachel: One option is to allocate the ventilator to Emily, the vaccinated mother of two.

> **Pros**: This decision aligns with the principle of rewarding responsible public health behavior and considers the societal impact of leaving two young children without a mother. It also avoids the moral hazard of encouraging non-compliance with public health guidelines.

> **Cons**: This could be seen as a form of punishment for Mark's personal choices, which some might argue should not be a factor in a life-or-death medical decision.

Prioritize Matt: Another option is to give the ventilator to Matt, despite his choice not to get vaccinated.

Pros: This would uphold the principle of medical neutrality, where care is provided irrespective of personal choices or societal opinions.

Cons: It risks public backlash and could be demoralizing for healthcare workers who have been advocating for vaccination. It also raises questions about the ethics of allocating scarce resources to those who have not taken preventative measures.

Random Selection: A third option is to randomly select who will receive the ventilator.

Pros: This eliminates personal bias and arguably treats all lives as equally valuable.

Cons: It may not be seen as the most ethical choice when considering the broader societal impact and could be emotionally devastating for the healthcare team.

Utilitarian Approach: Allocate the ventilator based on who is most likely to benefit from it, considering factors like age, overall health, and potential for recovery.

Pros: This approach aims to maximize overall well-being and could be seen as the most "rational" choice.

Cons: It opens up the Pandora's box of ethical questions about the value of a life, and who gets to make that judgment.

Defer to an Ethical Committee: The healthcare team could defer the decision to an institutional ethics committee or similar body.

> **Pros**: This would distribute the ethical burden and ideally involve experts in ethical decision-making.

> **Cons**: Given the time-sensitive nature of the situation, waiting for a committee decision could be impractical and result in loss of life.

Each of these options presents a unique set of ethical challenges and implications, making the decision far from straightforward. The healthcare team must weigh the pros and cons carefully, considering not only the immediate impact but also the long-term consequences for all stakeholders involved.

Ethical Analysis

Before diving into the ethical analysis, it's crucial to remember that the Hagakure's wisdom serves as a guiding light in this complex maze of moral choices. The ancient text teaches us to make decisions "within the space of seven breaths," urging us to be both decisive and ethically sound. As we explore the various options through the lenses of utilitarianism, deontology, virtue ethics, and care ethics, let's keep this samurai wisdom in mind. It's not just about making a quick decision; it's about making the right one. Now, let's examine each option in detail.

Prioritize Rachel:

> **Utilitarianism**: This option aims to maximize overall happiness by considering the societal impact of Rachel's survival. Her role as a mother and her responsible behavior in getting vaccinated could be seen as contributing to greater societal good.

> **Deontology**: From a duty-based perspective, prioritizing Emily could be seen as rewarding responsible behavior, thereby fulfilling a moral obligation to promote public health.

> **Virtue Ethics**: This choice aligns with virtues like responsibility and foresight, as Emily took preventative measures to protect herself and others.

> **Hagakure Guidance**: "In the words of the ancients, one should make his decisions within the space of seven breaths." This option might align with the Hagakure's emphasis on decisive action that aligns with societal values and responsibilities.

Prioritize Mall:

> **Utilitarianism**: This option may not maximize overall happiness, given the potential demoralization of healthcare workers and public backlash.

> **Deontology**: From a duty-based perspective, providing care irrespective of personal choices aligns with the principle of medical neutrality.

Virtue Ethics: This choice could reflect virtues like compassion and impartiality.

Hagakure Guidance: The Hagakure might see this as a test of one's resolve to uphold ethical principles, even when they are unpopular or difficult to implement.

Random Selection:

Utilitarianism: This option may not maximize overall well-being, as it leaves the decision to chance rather than considering broader impacts.

Deontology: Random selection could be seen as the most impartial method, fulfilling a duty to treat all lives as equally valuable.

Virtue Ethics: This could reflect the virtue of fairness but may lack in prudence and wisdom.

Hagakure Guidance: The Hagakure might question the wisdom of leaving such a critical decision to chance, suggesting that decisive action is needed.

Utilitarian Approach:

Utilitarianism: By definition, this approach aims to maximize overall well-being.

Deontology: This could conflict with a duty-based approach that argues all lives are equally valuable.

Virtue Ethics: This choice could reflect virtues like wisdom and prudence but might be seen as lacking in compassion or fairness.

Hagakure Guidance: The Hagakure might support this approach as it requires a decisive action based on a thoughtful consideration of the outcomes.

Defer to an Ethics Committee:

Utilitarianism: This could maximize well-being by involving ethical experts, but the time delay could result in negative outcomes.

Deontology: Delegating the decision could be seen as fulfilling a duty to ensure the most ethical choice is made.

Virtue Ethics: This could reflect virtues like humility and wisdom in acknowledging the complexity of the decision.

Hagakure Guidance: The Hagakure might criticize this option for its potential to cause delays, advocating instead for decisive action.

In summary, each option has its merits and drawbacks when viewed through different ethical lenses. The Hagakure's guidance on making decisions "within the space of seven breaths" serves as a reminder that, in high-stakes situations, decisiveness is a virtue—but one that must be balanced with ethical deliberation.

Recommended Course of Action

This case study is the very definition of Embracing Challenges! After a thorough ethical analysis, the most balanced course of action would be to implement a triage system that prioritizes care based on medical need, but also takes into account other ethical considerations such as social responsibility and fairness. This approach aligns most closely with the principles of utilitarianism, aiming to do the most good for the most people, while also honoring the deontological duty to treat each patient as an end in themselves.

In the spirit of the Hagakure, this decision is made "within the space of seven breaths," not as a rushed judgment, but as a decisive action that breaks through the ethical complexities to arrive at a solution. It embodies the samurai's resolve to face challenges head-on, without being paralyzed by the weight of the dilemma.

This recommendation also respects the virtue ethics principle of cultivating good character traits such as fairness and compassion. It acknowledges the care ethics perspective by considering the relational aspects of healthcare, ensuring that the system is not just efficient but also empathetic.

In summary, this course of action attempts to harmonize the conflicting ethical principles and stakeholder interests, offering a nuanced yet decisive solution to the complex issue of healthcare rationing during times of scarcity. It's a decision that, while difficult, aims to uphold the highest ethical standards in the face of unprecedented challenges.

Conclusion

The case of healthcare rationing during times of scarcity, such as a pandemic, presents a labyrinth of ethical complexities. It forces us to confront uncomfortable questions about the value of human life, the responsibilities of healthcare providers, and the limitations of our medical system. We've navigated through a maze of conflicting duties, moral principles, and stakeholder interests, each adding layers of complexity to an already challenging ethical landscape.

The ethical issues at play here are not just theoretical exercises; they have real-world implications that can mean the difference between life and death. They test the mettle of healthcare providers, administrators, and policymakers, demanding not just medical expertise but ethical wisdom. It's a situation that calls for the kind of resolve and decisiveness espoused in the Hagakure, the ancient samurai text that serves as our ethical compass throughout this exploration.

Our recommended course of action, while not perfect, aims to strike a balance between competing ethical principles and stakeholder interests. It's a solution that requires courage, compassion, and a steadfast commitment to ethical integrity. And it's a decision that, once made, will need to be reflected upon, learned from, and perhaps even adjusted as new challenges arise. Because, in the end, ethical practice is not a destination but a continual journey—one that we must all undertake with the seriousness and resolve of a samurai facing battle.

In closing, this case study serves as a microcosm of the broader ethical challenges that healthcare providers face daily. It's a stark reminder that, in the world of healthcare, ethical dilemmas are not just occasional disruptions but inherent aspects of the work. And it's a call to action for all of us involved in healthcare to continually strive for ethical excellence, to embrace the challenges that come our way, and to face them with the wisdom and resolve of a true ethical warrior.

Chapter 7: The Way of the Ethical Clinician

'Matters of great concern should be treated lightly. Matters of small concern should be treated seriously.'

On the surface, it seems counterintuitive, doesn't it? Shouldn't we treat matters of great concern with the gravity they deserve? But let's dig a little deeper. What this ancient wisdom is nudging us toward is a mindset shift. In the high-stakes world of healthcare, where every decision can be a matter of life and death, the weight of 'great concerns' can paralyze us. But what if we approached them with the lightness of being, with the agility of a samurai who knows that hesitation could cost him his life?

Conversely, it's the 'small concerns,' the details, that often trip us up. These are the things we should scrutinize, treating them as seriously as a samurai treats the sharpening of his blade. Because it's the small oversights that can lead to big mistakes.

The Role of Intuition

Ah, intuition—the samurai's sixth sense, that gut feeling that whispers in your ear when there's no time for lengthy deliberation. It's like the samurai who senses an ambush before seeing it, who feels the wind shift and knows an arrow is coming. But how does this mystical sense translate into the high-stakes, fast-paced world of healthcare?

First, let's get one thing straight: intuition isn't some magical, unexplainable phenomenon. It's the culmination of experience, knowledge, and keen observation. It's your brain connecting dots faster than your conscious mind can keep up. You've seen this symptom before; you've dealt with this kind of ethical dilemma; you've read that journal article. All these pieces coalesce in a flash, guiding your hand, your words, your choices.

But when do you listen to this inner samurai? When do you trust this swift, silent counsel?

Here's the tricky part: intuition is a powerful tool, but it's not infallible. It's like a well-honed katana—deadly accurate but only as reliable as the hand that wields it. Your intuition can be clouded by stress, fatigue, or emotional turmoil. Ever heard of a samurai making a fatal error because his mind was elsewhere? Exactly.

So, how do you cultivate this ethical sixth sense? Practice, reflection, and more practice. Every ethical decision you make, every outcome you witness, adds a layer of polish to your intuitive lens. It's like the samurai who spends hours in the dojo, perfecting each strike until it becomes second nature. You engage in ethical discussions, you read case studies, you consult mentors. You immerse yourself in the ethical fabric of your profession until its threads weave seamlessly into your own.

When the moment comes, when you're faced with an ethical crossroads and there's no time to consult the scrolls—trust yourself. Your intuition is your internal Hagakure, a distillation of wisdom and experience that guides you when there's no time to think.

Remember, intuition isn't a substitute for ethical reasoning; it's a complement to it. After the dust settles, go back and analyze your decision. Was your intuition spot-on, or did it lead you astray? This reflective practice refines your intuitive skills, sharpening your sixth sense for the next ethical battle.

So, the next time you find yourself in the ethical trenches, listen for that whisper, that samurai in your soul. It might just be the ally you need!

Ethical Self Care

Picture a samurai stepping away from the fray, retreating to a quiet grove to meditate, to breathe, to reconnect with his inner warrior.

Ethical self-care isn't about spa days or weekend getaways—though those can be nice. It's about tending to your ethical well-being, ensuring that your moral compass stays true north even when storms rage around you. It's like the samurai who sharpens his sword, polishes his armor, and meditates on his code of honor. These acts of self-care aren't indulgences; they're necessities. They fortify his spirit for the battles ahead.

So, how do you recharge your ethical batteries? How do you maintain that moral resilience that's so crucial in the high-stakes world of healthcare?

First, let's talk about mindfulness. Remember that? The art of being present, of clearing the clutter from your mind so you can focus on the ethical task at hand. Make it a daily practice. Whether it's five minutes of deep breathing before your shift or a quick moment of gratitude before bed, these pockets of mindfulness are your mini-retreats, your ethical pit stops.

Next, engage in ethical dialogue. You're part of a community of healthcare providers who share your ethical challenges.

Discuss cases, debate dilemmas, dissect decisions. This isn't just about learning from others; it's about reinforcing your own ethical framework, like a samurai sparring with his comrades to hone his skills.

And don't forget reflection. Remember the samurai meditating in his quiet grove? That's you, reflecting on your ethical decisions, dissecting them, learning from them. This reflective practice is your ethical dojo, your training ground for the moral challenges that lie ahead.

But what about those times when the weight of ethical decisions starts to wear you down? When you feel like you're teetering on the edge of ethical burnout? That's when you pull out the big guns of self-care: seek mentorship, consult with ethicists, or even consider ethical supervision. These are your ethical sensei, your guides in the complex landscape of healthcare ethics.

If you feel your ethical energy waning, remember the samurai's retreat. Step back, breathe, and tend to your ethical self. Your patients, your colleagues, and your own moral integrity will thank you.

Balancing Empathy and Detachment

The Samurai's Heart—a poetic paradox of steel and softness, a delicate equilibrium between empathy and detachment. Imagine a samurai on the battlefield, his eyes locking onto those of his opponent. In that moment, he understands the other's fear, the weight of the life hanging in the balance.

Yet, he also knows he must wield his sword with unflinching resolve. How does he do it? How does he balance the yin of empathy with the yang of detachment? And what can we, as healthcare providers, learn from this?

Let's start with empathy, that warm, fuzzy feeling that makes us human, that connects us to our patients on a deeply personal level. Empathy is the emotional currency of healthcare, the foundation upon which trust is built. It's like the samurai's understanding of his opponent's emotions—a vital tool in the ethical toolkit. Without empathy, you risk becoming a healthcare robot, mechanically performing tasks without understanding the human impact.

But here's the catch: too much empathy can cloud your judgment, make you biased, and lead you down the slippery slope of ethical ambiguity. It's like a samurai so consumed by empathy that he hesitates, even for a split second, and that hesitation could cost him the battle.

Enter detachment, the counterbalance to empathy. Detachment doesn't mean you're cold or uncaring; it means you have the ability to step back, to see the bigger ethical picture. It's the samurai's unflinching resolve, his ability to make the tough call even when his heart is heavy. In healthcare, this could mean making end-of-life decisions, allocating scarce resources, or even reporting a colleague for unethical behavior. Detachment equips you to make these decisions with a clear head, guided by ethical principles rather than emotional impulses.

How do you strike this balance? How do you cultivate a clinician's heart?

First, practice mindfulness. Yes, we're back to that again. Mindfulness helps you become aware of your emotional triggers, your biases, and your ethical blind spots. It's like the samurai who meditates before battle, attuning himself to his emotional landscape.

Second, engage in ethical reflection. After an emotionally charged case, take a step back. Examine your decisions, your feelings, your ethical reasoning. Were you too empathetic? Too detached? This reflective practice helps you recalibrate your ethical balance, fine-tuning it for future challenges.

And finally, seek ethical mentorship. Sometimes, the balance between empathy and detachment is too complex to navigate alone. You need a seasoned guide, an ethical sensei, to help you find your way. Whether it's a senior colleague, an ethics committee, or a moral philosophy book, find your ethical north star and use it to guide you.

The clinician's heart, a balanced blend of empathy and detachment. It's not an easy path, but then again, the way of the samurai never was. Master this balance, and you'll not only be an effective healthcare provider; you'll be an ethical force to be reckoned with.

The Ethical Clinician's Toolkit

Every clinician has a toolkit, even if it's not filled with swords and spears. In the realm of healthcare, your toolkit is metaphorical, but no less crucial. It's stocked with ethical principles and practices that you'll wield with the skill of a seasoned warrior. So, what's in this toolkit? Let's break it down.

Mindfulness: Clinical Focus

Remember the concept of "monkey mind"? It's the frenetic foe of ethical decision-making, swinging wildly from anxiety to distraction. In the clinician's toolkit, mindfulness is your meditation stone, a grounding element that brings you back to the present moment. Before making any weighty ethical decision, take a pause to breathe, center yourself, and settle those shrieking inner primates.

It's like a samurai taking a purposeful breath before drawing his sword - though hopefully less dramatic! This mindful reset allows you to act from a place of clarity, not reactionary chaos. Without it, you're at the mercy of the hyperactive monkeys within. And let's be honest - would you trust an ethics dilemma to a grape-throwing simian?

So be prepared to gently herd those unruly monkey minds back into focus. Visualize leading them slowly into a peaceful meadow of introspection, away from the anxiety-inducing edge of ethical precipices. They may resist at first, but with practice you can cultivate stillness amidst their instinctual chaos.

Sure, the samurai in Hagakure had the luxury of a neatly codified life allowing ample time for contemplation. You, on the other hand, are juggling back-to-back patients plus your own inner primate pandemonium! But don't let that discourage you. Even a 30 second mindful reset between cases can work wonders.

Think of it like a momentary meditation-powered cage for your screaming inner monkeys. The results? Ethical decisions guided by level-headed wisdom, not impulse. Now take a breath, picture those monkeys calmly resting, and carry on with clarity! The healthcare hurdles await, but your mind is ready.

Justice: The Clinician's Guiding Light

Justice isn't just an abstract ideal - it's a practical beacon guiding you through the murky waters of healthcare ethics. But rather than envision it as a samurai's sword, picture justice as a glow-in-the-dark morality compass.

When faced with an ethical dilemma, consult your trusty neon compass. Its radiant arrows will point towards the true moral north of fair and equitable treatment. Let its bright colors illuminate potential pitfalls, allowing you to navigate to the safest ethical shores.

Will this magical moral compass actually manifest in glowing plastic form? Probably not. But imagining one can make the concept of justice more friendly and approachable. We all get lost sometimes, whether in a dark forest or the swirling complexities of ethics. Visualizing a guiding light helps us stay on the right path.

So rather than wielding justice like a severe sword, try carrying it gently as a glowing compass. Its soft illumination feels more human and understanding than stark steel. But it still guides you firmly towards moral truth north, even on the cloudiest of ethical days.

Honor: The Clinician's Armor

Picture honor not as a suit of heavy samurai armor, but as a lightweight yet impervious super scrubs protecting both you and the institution you represent. When you act ethically, you're not just safeguarding your own integrity; you're upholding the moral standards of your entire healthcare organization.

Before taking any action, consider its impact on your honor suit. Will it add an unseemly stain, or make the fabric shine brighter? It's like a clinician-turned-superhero polishing their colorful spandex suit, aware that its condition reflects on their entire healthcare lineage.

Granted, the mental image of clinicians in candy-colored super scrubs may seem farfetched. But imagining honor as a protective second skin can help make ethics feel less like a burdensome suit of armor. Rather than a weighty duty, it becomes an empowering chance to show one's heroic colors!

So next time you face an ethical crossroads, picture yourself standing tall in your principles, flexible ethics fabric allowing you to gracefully navigate any moral dilemma. Your honor suit makes you ethics-minded yet approachable, upholding institutional integrity with a hint of lightheartedness. Time to flaunt your ethical style - the patients need you!

Resilience: The Clinician's Endurance

Resilience is not just rations, but a secret stash of snacks sustaining you through long days of ethical quandaries. It's what fuels you to face challenge after challenge without losing your moral compass. How do you build this stash? Stock up on bites of wisdom gained through reflection on tough cases. Replenish reserves by boldly diving into new dilemmas head-on.

It's like a samurai warrior training harshly, but taking occasional breaks for sushi and mochi to maintain sanity. Even ronin need real food for the marathon, not just metaphorical "rations!"

So be sure to keep your resilience stash fully loaded with plenty of ethical and emotional snacks. Harvest wisdom from past challenges, but balance it out with self care to avoid burnout. After a long day untangling ethical knots, recharge with a rejuvenating dessert, not just dry ruminating. You've earned a treat!

Building resilience takes perseverance, but don't let the martial metaphors make it feel too grim. Lighten the long battle with little ethical pick-me-ups along the way. Before charging the next moral mountaintop, take a meditative break for morale-boosting dumplings.

The Ethical Compass: Your Personal Code

Rather than envision your ethical code as an abstract guiding compass, picture it as the moral equivalent of a trusty GPS. When you're lost in a maze of ethical uncertainty, this handy gadget provides a route back to true north.

Program it with your core values - honesty, empathy, courage. Input destinations like "Maintain patient dignity" and "Uphold institutional honor." Now when ethical forks in the road arise, consult your moral GPS for the best route forward.

Of course, no GPS is 100% infallible. Technical glitches can occur, like when ethical ambiguity leads to the dreaded "Recalculating route..." message. But stay the course, and your values will eventually navigate the way.

Also, don't get distracted trying to change the programmed voice on your moral GPS to Morgan Freeman or SpongeBob. Fun as it might be to imagine ethics wisdom intoned by celebrities, resist temptation! Custom sound effects could make light of serious dilemmas.

But an occasional bit of guidance in Yoda's backwards speak is permissible: "Uphold patient autonomy you must!" Just enough silly to ease tension, while still providing direction. Everything in moderation.

At the end of the day, look at your ethical GPS as a useful support, not a rigid rulebook. Let it guide you down the right roads, but don't hesitate to occasionally forge your own path when the situation calls for it.

Empathy: The Clinician's Heart

Forget about envisioning empathy as a samurai's battle skill. Picture it instead as a superpower straight out of a comic book! With this amazing ability, you can leap into patients' perspectives in a single bound, understand their worries and motivations faster than a speeding stethoscope.

Empathy gives you an almost Spidey-sense for patients' emotions. It helps you anticipate fears and hopes, guiding your actions like Spiderman's precognitive Spidey-Sense tingles. You'll be wielding healthcare wisdom with the power and precision of Captain America's shield toss.

This emotional super-insight empowers ethical decision making with the force of Thor's hammer. When dilemmas arise, tap into your secret superpower. Feel the situation as the patient does. Let this empathy elevate your choices.

Sure, the hyperbolic superhero metaphor is a bit over the top. But imagining empathy as a legendary power can help build appreciation for this profound gift. It's a pivotal part of ethical healthcare, yet often overlooked. If we visualize it as amazingly impactful as a Marvel super-ability, it cements its proper place among key clinical skills.

So see your empathy as the greatest superpower of all - the power to profoundly understand. Use it wisely, let it guide your hands and heart. With great emotional insight comes great ethical responsibility. Go forth and be an empathy hero!

Transparency: The Clinician's Arrows

Imagine transparency as a quiver of arrows representing truth and openness. Much like a skilled archer carefully selecting the right arrow before taking aim, you must thoughtfully determine what information to make transparent in any given situation.

Some arrows in your quiver embody transparency towards patients - explaining treatment options clearly, admitting when mistakes occur. Others represent openness with colleagues - voicing concerns, allowing respectful critiques. More arrows signify transparency with the public - communicating data on outcomes, owning up to past failings.

As with archery, ethical transparency requires practice and discernment. You must gauge variables like distance and conditions to choose the right arrow from your quiver for each unique target. Take careful aim, then let transparency fly swift and true towards its goal.

Of course, full transparency isn't always possible or wise. Some arrows may need to be held in reserve to avoid causing harm. But when in doubt, opt for greater openness. And if your arrow misses the mark, apologize sincerely and try again.

So be discerning yet bold in wielding your ethical quiver. New arrows will be added with experience and guidance. Train until your aim is true. Transparency takes courage, but with time will hit the bullseye of integrity.

Moral Courage: The Clinician's Grit

Moral courage is your battle cry, your inner voice that shouts "Charge!" when others whisper "Retreat." It's the ability to stand up for what's right, even when it's easier to look the other way. Think of it as the samurai's indomitable spirit, the fire that fuels his every action. When faced with ethical dilemmas that require tough calls, your moral courage is what pushes you to make the right choice, even at great personal cost.

Accountability: The Clinician's Acts

Forget the samurai's solemn ledger as a symbol for accountability. Instead, picture it as an upbeat ethics vlog, reviewing your moral dilemmas candidly yet lightheartedly.

Each day, take a moment for self-reflection. Pull out your imaginary video camera and get ready to hit record on the day's ethical highs and lows. Share your thought process transparently and own decisions that missed the mark. Let the camera capture both wisdom gained and flubs to avoid repeating.

Approach this vlog with a sense of humor. Laughter takes the sting out of admitting mistakes. And don't take yourself too seriously - even master clinicians face failures! Keep it fun and engaging as you chronicle the ongoing journey toward ethical growth.

At the end of each video, remind yourself that tomorrow brings renewed opportunity to put lessons learned into practice. The challenges ahead seem less daunting knowing you have a community of fellow clinicians tuning in for support.

So be accountable not just through stern self-evaluation, but also with uplifting honesty and wit. Let your ethics vlog chronicle the ups, downs, and humor that color an imperfect yet earnest striving for moral clarity. The bloopers will be learning moments too!

Ethical Dialogue: The Clinician's Council

Rather than a stoic samurai council, picture your ethical dialogue platform as a lighthearted support group, gathering around a circle of beanbag chairs to unpack dilemmas.

Here you can share your experiences and concerns without judgement, receiving empathy and reassurance. Discuss complex issues openly even when there are no easy answers. Find solace in knowing you all share similar struggles.

Lean into moments of levity and camaraderie - laughter is the best medicine, after all! Enjoy snacks and silly stress-relieving activities too. You deserve occasional moments of fun after wrestling with such thorny topics.

See this group as your oasis of understanding amidst the harsh ethical desert. It offers a wellspring of wisdom but also emotional nourishment. You'll leave each meeting replenished and ready to put insights into action.

Of course, while lighthearted, these meetings require courage and honesty. But the beanbag chairs cushion the discomfort of admitting uncertainty. And the group's support propels you forward, stronger for having connected.

The Art of Reflection

Forget the solemn samurai ritual - picture reflection instead as a quirky art form, like finger painting your ethical insights across a canvas.

Grab some moral dilemmas and a few cups of wisdom. Now slosh them recklessly together, letting colors of understanding blend and drip. Don't hesitate to get messy! Swirl your brush with abandon.

Stand back occasionally to see what shapes emerge. What new connections become visible? Dive back in to heighten vivid hues of virtue. It may seem chaotic at first, but keep layering - your ethical insight mural will take form.

Does finger painting offer the same depth as traditional reflection? Of course not. But this playful approach lowers the barrier to entry, makes introspection seem less intimidating. Experimenting openly helps overcome resistance to vulnerability.

So grab an ethical dilemma and start splattering. Toss textbook techniques - get creative! No need for perfection, this is an art of self-discovery. Embrace the messiness, see where the colors run. Those happy accidents will illuminate untapped wisdom within.

Reflection takes many forms. But don't forget the value of play. Embracing lightheartedness keeps heavy topics from weighing down your spirit. So fling that paint with purpose, and reflect freely!

How will you use these tools? Ah, that's where the real artistry begins. **It's one thing to own a sword; it's another to wield it like a master.**

The Cycle of Continuous Improvement

Reflection feeds into a cycle of continuous ethical improvement. Each time you reflect, you add another layer to your ethical understanding, another nuance to your decision-making skills. It's like a samurai who, after each battle, adds another layer of polish to his sword, making it sharper, more resilient.

The Role of Mentorship

In the world of samurais, mentorship is invaluable. A seasoned warrior imparts not just techniques but also wisdom, a deeper understanding of the warrior's path. In healthcare, seek out ethical mentors who can guide your reflective practice, offering insights that you might have missed. It's like a samurai sitting at the feet of an elder, absorbing wisdom that can only come from years of experience.

The Community of Reflective Practitioners

You're not a lone samurai; you're part of a community of healthcare providers who are all on their own ethical journeys. Share your reflections with this community. Engage in ethical dialogue, challenge each other, and celebrate the shared victories. It's like a gathering of samurais around a campfire, each sharing tales of battles won and lessons learned.

So, are you ready to step into your ethical dojo? Are you prepared to engage in the disciplined art of reflection, to spar with your "What Ifs," and to continuously polish your ethical sword? Remember, the path of the ethical clinician is not a sprint; it's a lifelong journey. And every journey is richer with a bit of reflection.

The Ethical Ripple Effect

Never underestimate the impact of your ethical choices. They ripple outwards, affecting not just you and your immediate circle, but your institution and the broader healthcare community. It's like the samurai's code of Bushido, which doesn't just guide his actions but shapes his legacy. What ethical legacy will you leave?

Legacy

Your ethical legacy encapsulates the enduring impact of ethical clinical practice. Picture a samurai's sword, passed down through generations, each scratch and nick telling a story of battles fought and values upheld. Now, imagine your ethical decisions as that heirloom, a legacy that reverberates through time, shaping not just individual lives but entire communities.

First, let's talk about the immediate impact—your patients. Every ethical decision you make leaves an imprint on their lives. Choose wisely, and you're not just healing them; you're also instilling trust, reinforcing the sacred patient-provider relationship. It's like a samurai who wields his sword with honor, earning the respect and loyalty of those he protects. But the impact doesn't stop there. Oh no, it ripples outward, like a stone tossed into a pond.

Next, consider your institution. Your ethical decisions contribute to its moral fabric, shaping its policies, its reputation, and its culture. It's akin to a samurai whose honor reflects on his clan, elevating its status and influence. Act ethically, and you become a role model, inspiring colleagues to uphold similar standards. You help create an environment where ethical practice is the norm, not the exception. And in today's world, where institutions can be made or broken by public opinion, that's no small feat.

But why stop there? Your ethical legacy extends even further, reaching out to your community and society at large. It's like a legendary samurai whose deeds become folklore, teaching valuable lessons to future generations. Your ethical practice sets a precedent, influencing public perception of healthcare and shaping policy debates. It contributes to the collective ethical consciousness, raising the bar for what's considered acceptable, admirable, even exemplary.

And let's not forget the global impact. We live in an interconnected world, where a single tweet can spark a revolution, and a medical breakthrough in one country can save lives in another. Your ethical decisions, especially in research or public health, could have far-reaching implications, affecting people you'll never meet in places you'll never visit. It's the samurai whose legacy becomes an heirloom, treasured and emulated by warriors in distant lands.

So, how do you build this ethical legacy?

It starts with intentionality. Be mindful of the ethical weight of your decisions, recognizing their potential for long-term impact. It's the samurai who sharpens his sword with purpose, aware that it's not just a weapon, but a symbol of his values.

Next, engage in continuous ethical education. The landscape of healthcare ethics is ever-changing, and you need to stay updated to navigate it effectively. It's like a samurai who never stops training, always seeking to improve his skills and understanding.

And finally, mentor the next generation. Share your ethical wisdom, your experiences, your dilemmas. Help them build their own ethical toolkits, their own moral compasses. It's the samurai who trains young warriors, passing down not just his sword but also the principles that guide its use.

A legacy of ethical practice that transcends the here and now. It's a daunting responsibility, but also a profound opportunity. Seize it, and you'll leave behind something far more valuable than any material possession: an ethical legacy that shapes the future of healthcare. And that, my friends, is something worth fighting for.

The Final Stand

As you step out into the complex, ever-changing landscape of healthcare ethics, remember the Hagakure's wisdom. Treat matters of great concern lightly and matters of small concern seriously. It's not just a philosophy; it's a strategy, a way of navigating the world that turns challenges into opportunities for ethical growth. And in doing so, you become not just a healthcare provider, but a true ethical clinician, a samurai in scrubs.

Conclusion

'A samurai will use a toothpick even though he has not eaten.'

A samurai will always have a toothpick on hand, even if he hasn't had a bite. Odd habit, you might think! But, it's all about being ready for anything, any time. It's basically the samurai version of "Always be prepared," but with a slight dental hygiene twist I suppose.

In the context of healthcare, this could be interpreted as the importance of always being prepared, both in knowledge and in ethical grounding. Even when you're not in the midst of an ethical dilemma or a medical emergency, the disciplined, ongoing practice of ethical principles and medical knowledge can prepare you for the challenges that will inevitably come. It's a call to constant vigilance and continuous improvement, to never let your ethical or professional guard down. Just as a samurai with a toothpick is always ready, so too should healthcare providers be ever prepared to meet the ethical and professional challenges that come their way, often like a ninja in the night.

Summary of Key Insights

We've spelunked through the about-as-fun-as-it-sounds labyrinth of modern medical ethics, armed only with the wisdom of Zen Buddhism, Bushido, and the Hagakure. You know, that light reading you keep on your bedside table. We've tackled everything from the sheer joy of decisiveness to the delightful complexities of loyalty, and even tiptoed along the tightrope of balancing compassion and justice. It's been like a theme park – if the theme was 'ancient ethics meet modern dilemmas.'

But, wait! There's more. These principles aren't just for when you're playing doctor in the hospital or clinic. They're not some kind of ethical superhero costume you put on with your scrubs or white coat. No, my friend, they're more like your underwear – essential, everyday wear. And just like you wouldn't go out without your underwear, these principles are there for you in every walk of life. Whether you're wrestling with ethical dilemmas in healthcare, or just trying to figure out who gets the last slice of pizza at home, these principles are your trusty compass. They're as relevant to your interactions with your family, your friends, and that guy who always takes your parking spot, as they are to those adrenaline-fueled moments in the ER.

That mindfulness you've been flexing while making ethical decisions about Mrs. Johnson's care? It doesn't clock out when you do. It's there to make you a less forgetful spouse, a parent who actually knows the name of your kid's favorite toy, or a friend who remembers that Carol is allergic to peanuts... before you hand her a peanut butter sandwich.

And that delicate ballet between compassion and justice you're always practicing in healthcare? It's the same two-step you're doing when you're playing judge in the epic battle of "He took my toy!" between your kids. Or deciding who gets the last grant in your community work - the local park or the senior center.

The honor and integrity you parade around in your professional life? They aren't just for show. They're like your personal ethical brand label, influencing how your community sees you - "Oh, that's Pat, always does the right thing." It's even shaping how you see yourself when you look in the mirror each morning.

In essence, being an ethical clinician isn't something you can switch on and off like a rerun of your favorite medical drama. It's more like a 24/7 reality TV show, with you as the star. It's the road you're traveling every day, even if sometimes it feels like you're stuck in traffic. It's the background music to your life, influencing not just your professional choices, but also shaping your character, your relationships, and ultimately, your legacy. So, keep going, and remember: the ethical path might be a marathon, not a sprint, but at least you're running in the right direction.

Ethical Behavior: A Call to Action

The idea that ethical practice is a destination is about as accurate as saying a samurai's training ends when he gets his first sword. Or that you've mastered cooking the moment you boil water without burning down the kitchen. In reality, the journey is ongoing, a never-ending yellow brick road through the magical land of human interaction, professional challenges, and personal growth. Just as a samurai keeps his blade sharp and his ponytail tighter, we too must keep our ethical sensibilities in tip-top shape.

The principles we've dissected in this book—mindfulness, compassion, justice, honor, resilience—are not just items on a grocery list. They're virtues, qualities to be nurtured like a bonsai tree. Or a sourdough starter. Your call.

Think of these principles as seeds. Once planted, they need your tender loving care—watering, sunlight, the occasional pep talk—to grow and flourish. They demand your attention, like a needy cat at 3 AM, not just in your professional life but in every nook and cranny of your existence. And as you care for these seeds, you'll find they start popping up in places you least expected. Your heightened sense of justice might turn you into a local superhero, your cultivated mindfulness could make you the star of your next family reunion, and your honed resilience may help you face your mother-in-law's critique like a champ.

What's more, the ethical landscape changes faster than a teenager's mood, just like the seasons a samurai must adapt to. New gadgets, changing social norms, and emerging ethical brain teasers ensure that your ethical toolkit needs to be as flexible as a yoga instructor. Your understanding of these principles will deepen, kind of like those laugh lines around your eyes, as you gain more experience, face new challenges, and grow both professionally and personally.

So, as you close this book, don't consider it the end. Think of it as a milestone on your ongoing journey, a rest stop where you've refueled and re-armed for the challenges ahead. Whether you're in the operating room or the living room, remember that every moment presents an opportunity to practice these principles. And in doing so, you're not just a healthcare provider; you're a human being striving for ethical excellence, a modern-day samurai mastering the art of living.

Now, go forth and live your "Seven Breaths" moments, both in healthcare and in life, with the wisdom and courage of a seasoned samurai!